Delilah's
FIRST ANNUAL
Rock 'n' Roll
HANDBOOK

**A DELILAH BOOK** DISTRIBUTED BY THE PUTNAM PUBLISHING GROUP
NEW YORK

DELILAH'S FIRST ANNUAL
ROCK'N'ROLL HANDBOOK

Copyright © by Delilah Communications, Ltd.

A DELILAH BOOK

Delilah Communications, Ltd.
118 East 25 Street
New York, New York 10010

ISBN: 0-88715-002-0
Library of Congress Catalog Card Number: 84-45295

Manufactured in the U.S.A.
First Printing 1984

All rights reserved. No part of this book may be reproduced
or transmitted in any form or by any means, electronic or
mechanical, including photocopying, recording
or by any information storage and retrieval system, without
permission in writing from the Publisher.

*Editorial Staff:* Arlene Schuster
　　　　　　　　Patty Matranga
*Book Design:* Virginia Rubel

## PERMISSIONS

Delilah Books respectfully acknowledges the following original sources, extracts from which comprise over 90% of the contents of this Delilah anthology: *George Martin Remembers The Beatles,* by Jeannie Sakol and *Who's Who On The Sgt. Pepper Cover* from THE COMPLEAT BEATLES, copyright © 1981 by Delilah Communications, Ltd./ATV Music Publications; *Phil Spector: The Man Behind The Girl Groups* from GIRL GROUPS: THE STORY OF A SOUND by Alan Betrock, copyright © 1982 by Alan Betrock; *Rock on Film* from ROCK ON FILM by David Ehrenstein and Bill Reed, copyright © 1982 by Delilah Communications, Ltd. *Elvis: The Final Summer* from ELVIS WE LOVE YOU TENDER by Dee Presley, Billy, Rick and David Stanley, as told to Martin Torgoff, copyright © 1979 by Dee Presley, Bill, Rick and David Stanley; *Walk Right Back: The Everly Brothers Reunion,* copyright © 1983 by Arena International Merchandising Services Ltd.; *Rock Quiz: Test Your Rock-Ability* by Jack Lechner from THE IVY LEAGUE ROCK AND ROLL QUIZ BOOK, copyright © 1983 by Jack Lechner. Additional material, quotes and factual adaptations are from THE BOOK OF ROCK QUOTES, copyright © 1982 by Omnibus Press and ROCK CHRONICLE by Dan Formento, copyright © 1982 by Dan Formento.

*Michael's Solo Career* by Caroline Latham appears in MICHAEL JACKSON THRILL, copyright © 1984 by Kensington Publishing Co. and reprinted with their permission.

# Table of Contents

GEORGE MARTIN REMEMBERS THE BEATLES    6

WHO'S WHO ON THE SGT. PEPPER COVER    11

ROCK SPEAK    13

PHIL SPECTOR: THE MAN BEHIND THE GIRL GROUPS    30

ROCK ON FILM    38

ROCK VIDEOS    70

ROCK BIRTHDAYS    72

ROCK DEATHS    104

ROCK MARRIAGES & DIVORCES    118

ROCK LISTS    124
ROCK & ROLL SINGLE ARTISTS, ROCK & ROLL BANDS, FOREIGN BANDS, BANDS OF THE EIGHTIES

ELVIS: THE FINAL SUMMER    128

BAD NEWS BLUES    134

WALK RIGHT BACK: THE EVERLY BROTHERS REUNION    143

ROCK QUIZ: TEST YOUR ROCK-ABILITY    148

---

SPECIAL BONUS FEATURE:
    MICHAEL JACKSON'S SOLO CAREER    164

# George Martin remembers The Beatles

George Martin was born in England in 1926. Trained as a classical musician, he studied the oboe with Margaret Asher, the mother of Jane and Peter. In 1950, he joined EMI Studios as an Artists and Repertoire man for Parlophone Records. On June 6, 1962, he auditioned The Beatles at EMI Studio 3 on London's Abbey Road, and on September 11 produced their first Parlophone recording, "Love Me Do." He produced every Beatles recording until they disbanded, and was also musical director for the soundtracks of such films as *A Hard Day's Night, Yellow Submarine, Live and Let Die,* and *Sgt. Pepper's Lonely Heart's Club Band.* His many awards include four Grammys and the Queen's Silver Jubilee Award for Best Producer 1952-1977.

**Date:** Friday, December 5, 1980
**Place:** George Martin's office at Chrysalis Records in a quiet *cul de sac* behind London's busiest thoroughfare, Oxford Street

It is three days before the grotesque event at the Dakota Apartments three thousand miles away in New York City, and the meeting with George Martin is recalled in the wistful retrospect of its innocence of the tragedy to come.

George Martin is in the midst of producing a new LP with Paul and Linda and Wings, the first time in eight years that he is working with McCartney. "Not that he really needs *me*," he smiles diffidently. "He's such a clever bloke—a melder of sounds, not a straight-ahead rock-and-roller. All that he needs from me is a person who can see the whole picture. And hear it. He trusts me not to give the psychiatric view."

One of nature's truly elegant men, he looks like the hero of a stiff upper lip movie set during World War II and, in fact, did serve as a flyer in the Royal Navy. Low key and courteous of manner, he conveys a sense of fierce integrity and gentle strength. Sitting opposite him over a morning cup of tea, the recipient of his full attention finds it easy to understand the emotional trust and professional confidence The Beatles felt for this extraordinary man.

Among his fondest Beatles memories this sunny Friday morning are the making of "Strawberry Fields Forever" and "Penny Lane." "Two masterpieces" is how American music critic Jack Kroll assessed them from the retrospect of 1981, asserting that they demonstrate McCartney and Lennon's greatest gifts as artists, "their genius blending images of Utopia and loss, a beautiful but tough idealism about reality and its way of dissolving into a dream."

Contrasting the surreal characters of Paul's "Penny Lane"—the barber, the banker, and the fireman beneath blue suburban skies — with John's "Strawberry Fields" school where he was taken to the annual garden party by his aunt Mimi, Kroll concluded, "These are great songs. If they are pop, then clearly pop is capable of greatness in expressing the gathering pathos of mass society."

George Martin remembers the day in November, 1966 when John first played "Strawberry Fields" for him and Paul. "I was sitting on my usual high stool and Paul was beside me. John stood before us with his acoustic guitar and sang it. It was absolutely lovely."

But something happened during the recording session. "It had somehow lost the gentle quality. It was good heavy rock which was something else."

Up to that time, The Beatles had never re-recorded anything. Spontaneous energy was central to the creative process. "We always thought that if it didn't work out the first time around, we shouldn't try it again."

As it turned out, John shared Martin's uneasiness and suggested the producer score something for trumpets and cellos to add a new dimension to the effort. It wasn't long before The Beatles were back in the studio to record a new, improved "Strawberry Fields Forever."

Now came the dilemma. John liked the beginning of the first cut and the end of the second. How would it be if George Martin simply joined the two parts together?

"There were two small problems," the producer remembers with obvious delight. "The two cuts were in different keys and different tempos."

Challenged by what seemed an insurmountable task, he listened to the two versions again and again, waiting for inspiration. Suddenly, he realized that the way the keys were arranged, the slower version was a semi-tone flat compared to the faster one.

"If I could speed up one and slow down the other, I could get the pitches the same and, with any luck, the tempos would be sufficiently close so one wouldn't notice the difference — I hoped!"

Using a variable control tape machine, he joined the two versions together. The combination worked and that's how it was released.

"Penny Lane" presented a challenge of a different kind. At a concert performance of Bach's *Brandenburg Concerto*, Paul had heard a piccolo trumpet and suggested The Beatles include the high piping instrument in the recording of "Penny Lane." The piccolo trumpet plays an octave above a traditional trumpet and is therefore half its length, almost like a toy, about ten inches long.

The ever-accommodating Martin hired David Mason of the London Symphony Orchestra to bring his piccolo trumpet and join the recording session.

"It was something that had never been done in rock before. Paul would decide which notes he wanted and I would write them down for David. The result was unique and it gave 'Penny Lane' a distinct character."

When it was decided to release both songs together as a single, there could be no B-side. Both were A-sides and were acclaimed and reviewed as such. In George Martin's estimation, "It was the best record we ever made." His only disappointment was that it failed to reach Number 1 on the charts during the first week of issue.

"Unlucky Thirteen" he still calls it, exactly thirteen years after the event. The twelve previous Beatles releases had soared instantly to top chart position: "Please Please Me," "From Me to You," "She Loves You," "I Want to Hold Your Hand," "Can't Buy Me Love," "A Hard Day's Night," "I Feel

Fine," "Ticket to Ride," "Help!," "Day Tripper," "Paperback Writer" and "Yellow Submarine."

Not that the double-A was exactly a failure. It zoomed to the Number 2 spot that first week. Ironically, the song that topped them was Englebert Humperdinck's "Release Me," produced by Peter Sullivan, who was to become George Martin's partner in later years.

A pioneer in the development of recording processes, George Martin's favorite description is to compare making a record to painting a picture with sound. "Orchestration is different from composition. Orchestration is what gives color to what's written. Composition is musical line and harmony. Whether it's performed on a synthesizer or by a hundred piece orchestra, it's still the basic composition. Orchestration is painting a picture with a subtle coloring and a three dimensional form. I get a mental picture of how the sound picture will turn out."

With "Yesterday," for example, he points out that they used orchestration for the first time and from then on progressed to whole new areas. This had two results. On the one hand, the increasing sophistication of the records meant that George Martin, producer, was having a greater influence, technical and otherwise, on the music and the final result.

But on the other hand, the personal relationship between him and The Beatles changed, too.

"At the start, I was like the master with his pupils and they did what I said. They knew nothing about recording, but heaven knows they learned quickly so that soon I was to become the servant and they the masters."

As to comparisons of The Beatles with such classical composers as Beethoven, Bach and Schubert, George Martin shrugs amiably. It's a subject he's frequently asked to comment upon. "Not the same category, of course, although Beethoven wrote for bands and Schubert could be said to have written 'pop' music in that his songs were sung for the pleasure of ordinary people. If Bach were alive today, I'm sure he'd be working at music in the same way that we do in the business today. Above all, he was a worker and a craftsman and he didn't enjoy much reverence in his time."

Where he would place The Beatles historically is in comparison with such American composers as George Gershwin, Cole Porter and Jerome Kern. "The Beatles' output is concentrated. They wrote nearly three hundred songs in ten years. Just remember that in Bach and Beethoven's time, the working class never heard of them. There was no such thing as music for the masses. Even in the 1930's you had to be able to afford Gershwin and Kern records and sheet music. In the 1960's, it was the first time in history that young people had the money and influence to start a musical revolution. The Beatles' music and lyrics are of their generation."

George Martin's assistant, Shirley Burns, has been holding calls but now there is one that cannot be postponed. Paul McCartney wants to schedule the afternoon recording session at the studio in Sussex for the LP-in-progress that will be interrupted by the trauma of John Lennon's death and only completed many desolate weeks later at George Martin's studios on the Caribbean island of Montserrat.

Since Martin's wife, Judy, and their children are at their country house, he has been staying on his own at their London flat. As he gets ready to leave for Sussex, a concerned and protective Shirley wants to know, "What time did you get back from the studio last night?"

"After midnight."

"Did you have your supper, then?"

Martin's manner becomes that of a guilty schoolboy. A man who could easily order-in a gourmet feast, he confesses to having cooked himself a "nursery tea" consisting of three rashers of bacon, baked beans on toast and a steaming mug of Horlicks, a malted milk concoction cherished by generations of British children.

The veteran producer's departure for the recording studio suddenly personalizes the statistical fact that this kind, self-effacing man was a crucial participant in the recording of over two hundred Beatles songs. The enormity of this prompts a final record collector's question.

"Do you have a complete set of all The Beatles records?"

A pause. A smile. "I have them all in my head."

# SGT. PEPPER

- Recording produced by George Martin
- Cover by MC Productions and the Apple
- Staged by Peter Blake and Jann Haworth
- Photographed by Michael Cooper
- Wax figures by Madame Tussaud's
- A splendid time is guaranteed for all

**WHO'S WHO IN SGT. PEPPER'S BAND**

The first "rock concept" album. *The* bridge between art and pop. *The* most famous pop album in history.

*Sgt. Pepper's Lonely Hearts Club Band* is known not only for its brilliant musical imagery and biting lyrics, but for the cover of assembled luminaries ranging from childhood heroes (Lawrence of Arabia, Livingstone) to nostalgic movie stars (Mae West, Fred Astaire, Tom Mix) to public figures (Karl Marx and C.G. Jung) to original Beatle Stu Sutcliffe. To say nothing of the Fab Four themselves! When asked about the origin of the cover, The Beatles replied, "We wanted to put on people we like!"

1. Guru (Indian Holy Man); 2. Aleister Crowley (The Beast 666—black magician); 3. Mae West; 4. Lenny Bruce (American comedian); 5. Stockhausen (Modern German composer); 6. W.C. Fields; 7. C.G. Jung (psychologist); 8. Edgar Allan Poe; 9. Fred Astaire; 10. Merkin (American artist); 11. Drawing of a girl; 12. Huntz Hall (Bowery Boy); 13. Simon Rodia (folk artist — creator of Watts Towers); 14. Bob Dylan; 15. Aubrey Beardsley (Victorian artist); 16. Sir Robert Peel (police pioneer); 17. Aldous Huxley (philosopher); 18. Dylan Thomas (Welsh poet); 19. Terry Southern (author); 20. Dion (American pop singer); 21. Tony Curtis; 22. Wallace Berman (Los Angeles artist); 23. Tommy Handley (wartime comedian); 24. Marilyn Monroe; 25. William Burroughs (author of *Naked Lunch*); 26. Guru; 27. Stan Laurel; 28. Richard Lindner (New York artist); 29. Oliver Hardy; 30. Karl Marx; 31. H.G. Wells; 32. Guru; 33. Stuart Sutcliffe (former Beatle who died before group became famous); 34. Drawing of a girl; 35. Max Miller; 36. Drawing of a girl; 37. Marlon Brando; 38. Tom Mix (cowboy film star); 39. Oscar Wilde; 40. Tyrone Power; 41. Larry Bell (modern painter); 42. Dr. Livingstone (in wax); 43. Johnny Weissmuller (former Tarzan); 44. Stephen Crane (Nineteenth-Century American writer); 45. Issy Bonn (comedian); 46. George Bernard Shaw (in wax); 47. Albert Stubbins (Liverpool footballer); 48. Guru; 49. Einstein; 50. Lewis Carroll; 51. Sonny Liston; 52., 53., 54., 55. The Beatles (in wax); 56. Guru; 57. Marlene Dietrich; 58. Diana Dors; 59. Shirley Temple (child star); 60. Bobby Breen (singing prodigy); 61. T.E. Lawrence (Lawrence of Arabia); 62. American Legionnaire.

WHO'S WHO IN SGT. PEPPER'S BAND

# ROCK SPEAK

- *I've always said that pop music is disposable and it is, and that's the fun of pop music. If it wasn't disposable, it'd be a pain in the fuckin' arse.*

  —Elton John

- *Forget about the tired old myth that rock 'n' roll is just making records, pulling birds, getting pissed and having a good time. That's not what it's all about.*

  —Pete Townshend

- *The music is all. People should die for it. People are dying for everything else, so why not the music?*

  —Lou Reed

- *There's a lot of things blamed on me that never happened. But then, there's a lot of things that I did that I never got caught at.*

  —Johnny Cash

- *I think rock 'n' roll is all frivolity — it should be about pink satin suits and white socks.*

  —Mick Jagger

- *Rock 'n' roll is not just music. You're selling an attitude, too. Take away the attitude and you're just like anyone else. The kids need a sense of adventure and rock 'n' roll gives it to them. Wham out the hardest and cruellest lyrics as propaganda, speak the truth as clearly as possible.*

  —Malcolm McLaren

- *I don't understand why people think it's so incredibly difficult to learn to play a guitar. I found it incredibly easy. You just pick a chord, go 'twang,' and you've got music.*

  —Sid Vicious

- *There are more clowns than good guys in music. British bands don't play as well as American bands. Rock 'n' roll is simply an attitude—you don't have to play the greatest guitar.*

  —Johnny Thunder, Heartbreakers

*David Byrne*

- *There are certain things I feel need to be done in terms of music and performance, and what these things amount to is that the world doesn't need another posturing clown yammering away about his 'baby.'*

  **—David Byrne,** Talking Heads

- *It really is fantastic conceit on behalf of the Establishment to imagine that any particular fragment of society is ever the true subject of a rock 'n' roll song.... The definition of rock 'n' roll lies here for me: If it screams for truth rather than help, if it commits itself with a courage that it can't be sure it really has, if it stands up and admits something is wrong but doesn't insist on blood, then it is rock 'n' roll.*

  **—Pete Townshend**

- *I never really did anything that outrageous on stage. The hanging had been done ten million times in every Western. The guillotine had been done since 1925 in vaudeville shows. It's just the fact that it had rock 'n' roll behind it that made it sound so damn notorious.*

  **—Alice Cooper**

- *Rock 'n' roll is a technological art.*

  **—Patti Smith**

- *Messages become a drag, like preaching. I think one of the worst possible beliefs is that pop stars know any more about life than anyone else. The thing to do is to move people, to really turn them on, to subject them to a fantastic experience, to stretch their imagination.*

  **—Nick Mason,** Pink Floyd

- *I don't see that rock 'n' roll should be a bad influence on anyone. It's just entertainment and the kids who like to identify their youthful high spirits with a solid beat are thus possibly avoiding other pursuits which could be harmful to them.*

  **—Bill Haley,** 1959

- *The stage is a holy place, you do not get up there and degrade it.*

  **—Gene Simmons,** Kiss

- *Don't interpret me. My songs don't have any meaning. They're just words.*

  **—Bob Dylan**

- *Pulling down your pants isn't rock 'n' roll.*
  　　　　　　　　　　　—**Sirius Trixon,** Motor City Bad Boys
- *It's not a matter of playing the right notes, is it? It's a feel.*
  　　　　　　　　　　　　　　　　　　　　—**Twiggy**
- *Rock music has to be naïve. And when you're no longer musically naïve, or socially naïve, or intellectually naïve, and you start to get a bit more worldly-wise, no way can you do that any more.*
  　　　　　　　　　　　—**Ian Anderson,** Jethro Tull
- *To me, the great success of any truly great rock song is related to the fact that people who couldn't really communicate in normal ways can quite easily communicate through the mutual enjoyment of rock music.*
  　　　　　　　　　　　　　　　—**Pete Townshend**
- *You know, the rock revolution did happen, it really did. Trouble was nobody realized.*
  　　　　　　　　　　　　　　　　—**David Bowie**
- *Rock 'n' roll is the music that inspired me to play music. There is nothing conceptually better than rock 'n' roll. No group, be it The Beatles, Dylan or The Stones have ever improved on 'Whole Lotta Shakin' for my money. Or maybe, like our parents, that's my period and I'll dig it and never leave it.*
  　　　　　　　　　　　　　　　　—**John Lennon**
- *I'll never get tired of playing this music. I'm never gonna stop playing it. I'll go on playing just as long as there are people to listen.*
  　　　　　　　　　　　　　　　—**Jerry Lee Lewis**
- *I was in the studio one day at 706 Union Avenue and my secretary noticed that young man going by, very shy, and he wanted to make this record for his mother's birthday.*
  　　　—**Sam Phillips,** head of Sun Records, on the arrival of Elvis Presley
- *The colleges have to be destroyed, they're dangerous. Doctors trying to cure the freaks while they gulp pills. Rushing with the music. It's the music that kept us all intact...kept us from going crazy. You should have two radios—in case one gets broken.*
  　　　　　　　　　　　　　　　　　—**Lou Reed**
- *I build more sandcastles in one lifetime than there are pyramids in Egypt.*
  　　　　　　　　　　　　　　　　—**Arlo Guthrie**
- *You can only live one dream at a time.*
  　　　　　　　　　　　　　　　　—**Diana Ross**

- *There are a lot of things you have to sacrifice. It all depends on how deep you want to get into whatever your gig is.*
   —Jimi Hendrix

- *Convicts are the best audiences I ever played for.*
   —Johnny Cash

- *So what if I live with straights. I have straight babies.*
   —Paul McCartney

- *True cheapness is exemplified by the visible nylon strings attached to the jaw of the giant spider.*
   —Frank Zappa

- *Too many people are obsessed with pop. The position of rock 'n' roll in our subculture has become far too important, especially in the delving for philosophical content.*
   —Mick Jagger

- *I'd rather be called a jar of peanut butter than a punk. We are one of the first bands to be called punks but the scene has degenerated into a bunch of fashion-conscious poseurs paying nose-bleed prices for ripped-up t-shirts.*
   —**Barrie Masters,** Eddie and the Hot Rods

- *The glorification of the working class has been going on for a long time. There's something to be said for some of it, but I think that, when they try to do it by trying to write simple songs, it's really backward.*
   —**Jerry Harrison,** Talking Heads

- *Nothing can really be better than waking up in the morning and everything is still the same as it was the day before. That's the best thing you can have in life, consistency of some kind.*
   —Pete Townshend

- *If you're a writer, it's like making a sandwich, there's no great thing in it.*
   —Donovan

- *You can't simply set out to 'make art'. You enjoy yourself first of all. I see myself as an entertainer because it's what I do best. If we should happen to make art, then it's only as a side product of entertaining.*
   —**Sting**(Gordon Sumner), Police

- *I love people. I love life. I'm happy to be alive. I'll never grow old. We're all brothers and sisters in one big family. We all have power. We're all full of beauty just waiting to explode. It's always springtime.*
   —Jonathan Richman

- I don't think you could anymore train a person to be a country music singer than you could train someone to have almond eyes.

  —Merle Travis

- Message songs, as everybody knows, are a drag. It's only college newspaper editors and single girls under fourteen that could possibly have time for them.

  —Bob Dylan

Bob Dylan

- In America, you watch TV and think that's totally unreal. Then, you step outside, and it's just the same.

  —Joan Armatrading

- We know a lot of people don't like us because they say we're scruffy and don't wash. So what! They don't have to come and look at us, do they? If they don't like me, they can keep away.

  —Mick Jagger, 1964

- I think the main point of the situation is that those pieces of plastic we did are still some of the finest pieces of plastic around.

  —Ringo Starr, on The Beatles' eternal popularity

- Elvis died when he went into the Army.

  —John Lennon

- We never sold millions of albums, but we did try to get a toehold. We did always plan on holding out, on making music we could put our names on. I'd like to think we never put out any real dogs, and that we never joined up, and that we got in some good licks, and played some music that will last and be remembered.

  —Levon Helm, The Band

17

- They say we are obscene and vulgar...but I don't let them hang us up...we just get excited by the music and carried away.
  —Jimi Hendrix

- We're another generation. They're rich and living in another world altogether... to them it's just another way of making money. They're not playing for the kids. They're not playing for us. To them it's just another nine-to-five job.
  —**Joey Ramone,** on Sixties rock Establishment

- It was not a happy childhood. I mean, when your father blows his head open, it's not funny.
  —Phil Spector

- Gram Parsons had it all sussed. He didn't stick around. He made his best work and then he died. That's the way I'm going to do it. I'm never going to stick around long enough to churn out a load of mediocre crap like those guys from the Sixties.
  —Elvis Costello

- Elvis looked so clumsy and totally uncoordinated back then. And this was the beauty of it — he was being himself. He had that little innocence about him and yet even then he had a little something that was almost impudent. He certainly didn't mean to be impudent, but he had enough of that, along with what he could convey, that he was just beautiful and lovely.
  —Sam Phillips

- I always thought the good thing about the guitar was that they didn't teach it in school.
  —Jimmy Page

- The Beatles' major accomplishment was getting the older generation interested in rock.
  —**Dick Clark,** guru of *American Bandstand*

- My brother Dennis came home from school one day and he said 'Listen you guys, it looks like surfing's going to be the next big craze and you guys ought to write a song about it.' Because, at that time, we were writing songs for friends and school assemblies.
  —**Brian Wilson,** on the launch of The Beach Boys

- Lots of people who complained about us receiving the MBE received theirs for heroism in the war — for killing people. We received ours for entertaining other people. I'd say we deserve ours more, wouldn't you?
  —John Lennon

- *The old are scared of us. They don't want the change. It makes them irrelevant to what's going on now and they know it.*
  —**Johnny Rotten,** Sex Pistols

- *My moment of stardom was at the Aldermaston marches.*
  —**Rod Stewart**

- *We were the youngest generation of moneyed people, and we were just bigger kids about it.*
  —**Mama Cass Elliot**

- *I'll take today's teenagers any day to the ruckus rousers and souvenir scalpers who made our lives miserable during the heyday of Goodman and Sinatra. The worst thing these kids do is feed sugar to the horses.*
  —**New York City cop,** 1959

- *When I got the famous haircut of 1974 or whenever, everyone said 'Oh, God, what did you do? You were so perfect, two brothers who had that sort of long, curly hair—great gimmick!' And no one would look me in the eye. Our manager was really upset. It was like I had murdered my mother or something.*
  —**Ron Mael,** Sparks

- *People say I made The Rolling Stones. I didn't. They were there already. They only wanted exploiting.*
  —**Andrew Loog Oldham**

- *I don't think New York did very much for Sid.*
  —**Malcolm McLaren,** suggesting that Sid Vicious be buried in Britain

- *If you can survive in this line of work, then you can survive in the jungle. I know I'm a mixed character, but it's horses for courses. If someone's being rough with you, you gotta be rough back.*
  —**Peter Grant,** manager of Led Zeppelin

- *When you get in the record business, someone gonna rip you anyway so that don't bother me. If you don't rip me, she gonna rip me, and if she don't rip me, he gonna rip me, so I'm gonna get ripped, so you don't be bothered by that, because people round you gonna rip you if they can.*
  —**Muddy Waters**

*Rod Stewart*

- *If Patty Hearst were on United Artists Records, she never would have been found.*
  —**Dean Torrence**

- *They always think you're some kind of puppet. Yes, I am a puppet. But what everyone doesn't realize is that I'm also the one who's pulling the strings.*
  —**Shaun Cassidy**

- *All those shoe salesmen who ran the music business really felt threatened by our very existence. But I never liked that Communist image from the outset, 'cos me being Jewish for one thing, I really hate those Commie bastards.*
  —**Sylvain Sylvain,** New York Dolls

- *You can't get The Monkees back together as a rock 'n' roll group. That would be like Raymond Burr opening up a law practice.*
  —**Mike Nesmith**

- *My job is to get that emotion into a record. We deal with the young generation, with people lacking identification, the disassociated, the kids who feel they don't belong, who are in the 'in-between' period in their lives.*
  —**Phil Spector**

- *You are on private property. There is no trespassing or loitering of any kind, by anyone under Section 8-610 BHMC. There is an armed guard on duty, trained dogs, in addition to the Bel Air Patrol and a burglar service. All violators will be prosecuted to the full extent of the law and will be subject to fine or imprisonment and grave danger for entering private property. You are here at your own risk and are hereby advised to leave immediately.*
  —**Notice on Phil Spector's front gates**

- *I never signed a contract with The Beatles. I had given my word about what I intended to do and that was enough. I abided by the terms and no one ever worried about me not signing it.*
  —**Brian Epstein**

- *Darling, we're broke. David has been robbed blind. There were millions but other people got them, not us. It's the usual story with pop musicians. David has taken people to court but in the end he found it too unbearable to get involved at that sort of game — it simply puts you on their level.*
  —**Angie Bowie,** in the Evening Standard, 1977

- *I gave The Beatles their first tour — I took them to Hamburg before they ever made a record. I gave Mick Jagger his first tour in this country. James Brown was with me. I put Joe Tex in business.*
  —**Little Richard**

- *I didn't set out to become a star. I don't think of myself as a star. I set out to become a singer. I would have sung no matter what. The star part is just something they made up in Hollywood in 1930.*

  —Linda Ronstadt

- *While I'm very intelligent, I'm no intellectual. All of my beliefs, political and otherwise, are very romantic. It's like me having a crush on Prince Charles. I don't know anything about him. I just think there's something sexy about him.*

  —Patti Smith

- *I wouldn't exist as a musician without the tape recorder. More than anything else, that is the instrument I play.*

  —Brian Eno

- *I want to be the Prime Minister of England some day.*

  —David Bowie

- *I am totally fascinated by the U.S. I love Mickey Mouse and I think people should be allowed to work as hard as they want so they can achieve a more comfortable lifestyle. To me, that's New York City and having twenty-four hour TV and seven foot TV screens. That's happiness to me.*

  —Gene Simmons, Kiss

- *Before I got into rock 'n' roll, I was going to be a dentist.*

  —Gregg Allman

- *I would rather retain the position of being a photostat machine with an image, because I think most songwriters are anyway.*

  —David Bowie

- *I never work on anything. Dedication is such a weird word after all, after Albert Schweitzer and people like that. That's dedication, when you give your whole life. No one dedicates themselves to anything now.*

  —Ringo Starr

- *I'm paranoid about eating out-of-town tuna fish sandwiches, so I don't think I can discuss being a star intelligently.*

  —Carly Simon

- *'Blue Suede Shoes' was the easiest song I ever wrote. Got up at 3:00 AM when me and my wife Velda were living in a government project in Jackson, Tennessee. Had the idea in my head, seeing kids by the bandstand so proud of their new city shoes—you gotta be real poor to care about new shoes like I did—and that morning I went downstairs and wrote out the words on a potato sack. We didn't have any reason to have writing paper around.*

  —Carl Perkins

- *I think I must be a victim of circumstances, really. Most of it's my own doing. I'm a victim of my own practical jokes. I suppose that reflects a rather selfish attitude. I like to be the recipient of my own doings. Nine times out of ten, I am. I set traps and fall into them.*

　　　　　　　　　　　　　　　　　　　　　　　　　　　—Keith Moon

- *I never wanted to be a train driver, I wanted to be the best guitar player in the world.*

　　　　　　　　　　　　　　　　　　　　　　　　　　　—Peter Frampton

- *We were a band who made it very big, that's all. Our best work was never recorded.*

　　　　　　　　　　　　　　　　　　　　　　　　　　　—John Lennon

- *All my records are comedy records.*

　　　　　　　　　　　　　　　　　　　　　　　　　　　—Bob Dylan

- *Responsibility, security, success mean absolutely nothing.... I would not want to be Bach, Mozart, Tolstoy, Joe Hill, Gertrude Stein or James Dean. They are all dead. The Great books've been written. The Great sayings have all been said.*

　　　　　　　　—**Bob Dylan,** from the sleeve notes to *Bringing It All Back Home*

- *I manage to look so young because I'm mentally retarded. Actually, I think the reason I don't look as I really am is because of the junk and the yoga. I'm not a Communist. I'm a Humanist. That's why I'm attracted to Lenin.*

　　　　　　　　　　　　　　　　　　　　　　　　　　　—Debbie Harry

- *I don't call myself a poet, because I don't like the word. I'm a trapeze artist.*

　　　　　　　　　　　　　　　　　　　　　　　　　　　—Bob Dylan

- *My ultimate vocation in life is to be an irritant. Not something actively destructive, but someone who irritates, who disorientates. Someone who disrupts the daily drag of life just enough to leave the victim thinking there's maybe more to it all than the mere humdrum quality of existence.*

　　　　　　　　　　　　　　　　　　　　　　　　　　　—Elvis Costello

*Elvis Costello*

- My music has a high irritation factor. You can't put it on and eat potato chips to it and invite the neighbours in for a barbecue. It's got 'prick' in it, and 'wop' and 'I'm gonna take off my pants.' I entertain, but I've got something to say.

—**Randy Newman**

- I don't like to be called Elvis the Pelvis ... I mean, it's one of the most childish expressions I ever heard coming from an adult. But, uh, if they want to call me that, I mean, there's nothing I can do about it.

—**Elvis Presley**

- My voice is like a house I'm keeping up. You don't just build a house and do nothing else to it. You're always washing the windows, painting, adding a room.

—**Ray Charles**

- Getting myself up in the morning, or should I say afternoon, is like picking at a scab.

—**Janis Joplin**

- The big difference between us and punk groups is that we like KC and the Sunshine Band. You ask Johnny Rotten if he likes KC and the Sunshine Band and he'll blow snot in your face.

—**Chris Frantz,** Talking Heads

- I've met all the women and I'll tell you—I'm more woman than any of them. I'm a real woman because I have love, dependability, I'm good, kind, gentle and I have the power to give real love. Why else would you think that such a strong man as David Bowie would be close to me? He's a real man and I'm a real woman. Just like Catherine Deneuve.

—**Iggy Pop**

- We're just a bunch of crummy musicians, really.

—**George Harrison,** radio interview, 1962

- I'm very misunderstood, you know. It's the price I have to pay. Beethoven and Michelangelo were misunderstood in their time, too. I'm not concerned about now, but when I leave this earth, I'll be appreciated.

—**Marvin Gaye**

- More and more, with every song I write, I try to record what I see and leave out what I think.

—**Tom Paxton**

- D'ya ever see on vacation a fat kid that's trying to swim around a pool? That's how I felt trying to sing with them.

—**Randy Newman,** on singing harmony tracks for The Eagles

- Probably, the biggest bringdown of my life was being in a pop group and finding out how much it was like everything it was supposed to be against.

   —**Mama Cass Elliot**

- I'm just gonna keep on rocking, 'coz if I start saving up bits and pieces of me like that, man, there ain't gonna be nothing left for Janis.

   —**Janis Joplin**

- Most everybody has written me off. Oh yeah, they all acted like they were proud for me when I straightened up. Some of them are still mad about it, though. I didn't go ahead and die so that they'd have a legend to sing about and put me in hillbilly heaven.

   —**Johnny Cash**

- Writers can say what they like about me. That I'm skinny, that I'm ugly, that I got pimples. I don't care. The only thing that disturbs me is when someone questions my integrity.

   —**Patti Smith**

- They say our stuff is corny. Well, lots of people eat corn. Our lines are realistic and frank.

   —**Mary-Ann,** The Shangri-Las

- If I wanted to get anything out of this business, it was never to have to go back and work in a factory again. But one thing I've learned is that money never buys you out of being working class. The middle classes never let you forget where you've come from.

   —**Roger Daltrey**

- I don't want to be the world's oldest living folk singer.

   —**Joan Baez**

- I do have a sense of humor, you know, which is something most people completely wash over when they deal with me….It's like, a lot of the stuff I say is true, but it's supposed to be funny.

   —**Patti Smith**

- My dad was very strict and taught me I must always respect my elders. I couldn't speak unless I was spoken to first by grown-ups. So I've always been very quiet.

   —**Jimi Hendrix**

- At bedtime, a stern word from their father is enough to send them running for help to their nurse.

   —**Linda Eastman McCartney,** on her children

- *I am the product of a haphazard musical environment which, I suppose, makes me a folk artist.*
  —**James Taylor**

- *When I was two feet off the ground, I collected broken glass and cats. When I was three feet off the ground, I made drawings of animals and forest fires. When I was four feet off the ground I discovered boys and bicycles.*
  —**Joni Mitchell**

- *When I was a kid, really small, I saw my brother go into the bathroom. I'll never forget it. I tried to do it too....I stood over the toilet and tried to 'do it' the same way. My mother came in and tried to explain. I was outraged and demanded to know if he did it why couldn't I? I'm twenty-three, and still haven't changed. I want to know why I can't do it all.*
  —**Suzi Quatro**

- *His pompadour was high and his hip action was wicked when Elvis was still a pimply kid mowing lawns in Memphis.*
  —**Little Richard,** described by Lillian Roxon

- *I graduate from high school in two years time, when I'm eighteen. What do I want to do when I leave? I'll be a star by then so I don't have to worry.*
  —**Rachel Sweet**

- *I always loved The Beatles, they were incredible. I remember having a fight in class with a girl who tore down her Beatles pictures when Dick Clark came along. I didn't speak to her for three weeks.*
  —**Lesley Hornsby,** a.k.a. Twiggy

- *Me and me Dad were going to a football match and me Dad came out in this old coat, and it was rough. It was an old black coat and he had outgrown it and me Mum said, 'You can't go out in that bloody old coat! Your son's a millionaire, you'll disgrace the street.'*
  —**Rod Stewart**

- *When I was sixteen, I had two choices—football or rock. I chose rock because it was less limiting. And it was more exciting and I got into music at a very early age. I went to my first rock concert when I was twelve. It was free, in Hyde Park, and The Nice, Traffic, Junior's Eyes and The Pretty Things were playing.*
  —**Mick Jones,** The Clash

- *I love Michael Jackson. The quality of his voice is fantastic. He's the only kid I really like in that respect. Michael Jackson had it when he was one.*
  —**Ringo Starr**

- *I'm really a religious person. I used to be a preacher. Went to the Assembly of God Bible School in Texas. I sure don't want to go to Hell. I pray to God I don't. I* think I'll probably go to Hell if I don't change my way of living. Give me that whiskey!

—Jerry Lee Lewis

- Clean living keeps me in shape. Righteous thoughts are my secret. And New Orleans home cooking.

—Fats Domino

- Pop is the perfect religious vehicle. It's as if God has come down to earth and seen all the ugliness that was being created and chosen pop to be the great force for love and beauty.

—Donovan

- If Jesus Christ came back today, he and I would get into our brown corduroys and go to the nearest jean store and overturn the racks of blue denim. Then we'd get crucified in the morning.

—Ian Anderson, Jethro Tull

- God sent me on earth. He send me to do something and nobody can stop me. If God want to stop me, then I stop. Man never can.

—Bob Marley

- We got this far on faith, and it's the only way we know. It's kind of like we were hand picked and put together. That's why we call our band the Creator's band, because He brought us together.

—Al McKay, Earth, Wind & Fire

- What is evil? I don't know how much people think of Mick as the Devil or as just a good rock performer. There are black musicians who think we are acting as unknown agents of Lucifer and others who think we are Lucifer. Everybody's Lucifer.

—Keith Richards

- You know, if God showed up tomorrow and said, 'What do you want to do,' yeah, if he said, 'Do you want to be President?' No. 'Do you want to be in politics?' No. 'What do you want?' I want to be a rhythm guitar player.

—Lou Reed

- With a person who is an alcoholic, as I am, you don't ever have one or two drinks. It doesn't work that way. I've never had two drinks in my life.

—Grace Slick

- Led Zeppelin's success may be attributable, at least in part, to the accelerating popularity of barbiturates and amphetamines — drugs that render their users most responsive to crushing volume and ferocious histrionics.

—Los Angeles Times

- *I don't drink anything on the rocks. Cold is bad for my throat. So it's always straight or in tea. Southern Comfort tastes like orange petals in tea. I usually get about a pint-and-a-half down me when I'm performing. Any more, and I start to nod out.*

—**Janis Joplin**

- *I was a teenage coffee addict. When I was younger, I always wanted it because adults were drinking it. But my dad, until I was fifteen, never let me drink it. Once I started, I wanted it always...it was such a great high, I didn't think it was real bad until I started getting shaky and having stomach aches. Sometimes I couldn't write my name on a check because my hands were shaking so much. Finally, I decided to go cold turkey.*

—**Debby Boone,** daughter of Pat

Linda Ronstadt

- *Running is the best, and I think the only, cure for depression. There have never been any drugs that I could take that would make depression go away.*

—**Linda Ronstadt**

- *People think I lead a dissipated life. That's not true. Drugs are a cheat. I can see it right away in the color of the skin, in the quality of the hair, the nails, the brilliance of the eyes. Look at me — do I look like a heroin addict?*

—**Bianca Jagger**

- *In my next incarnation, I want to become a dolphin...I think they're the creatures on earth at the moment. They've always got an undefinable glint in their eye and the way they carry on I find very appealing.*

—**Robert Palmer**

- *I wonder how long it is until sculpture becomes litter?*

—**Ian Dury**

- Rock 'n' roll doesn't have to be adolescent music. It's got to grow up, for Christ's sake! That's what I believe and that's what I'm putting into practice. Right now, I'm sitting back and waiting. In the last year I've eased up. Now I get so much more out of just looking at the sun.

—**Kevin Coyne**

- Being a star is kind of silly. I'd rather be looked on as a comrade.

—**Laura Nyro**

- The Indian's never going to get a damn thing till he goes out and scalps a few people. Then he'll get attention.

—**Ray Charles**

- Love is not a matter of counting the years—it's making the years count.

—**Wolfman Jack**

- Sex to me is a beautiful thing and shouldn't be abused. You shouldn't sleep with just anybody, you shouldn't sleep with anybody for money, you should sleep with somebody you really like and that's it. And it's not a power or control thing. That's what I don't like about sex. That's why I haven't slept with anyone for two years.

—**Poly Styrene,** X-Ray Spex

- Groupie? I was just a superfan. Another girl looking for romance.

—**Cherry Vanilla**

- I lived with someone once for two years. But I decided that to be married you had to make married music. And I'm not ready for that.

—**Bruce Springsteen**

- You can't blame John for falling in love with Yoko any more than you can blame me for falling in love with Linda. At the beginning I was annoyed with him, jealous because of Yoko and afraid about the breakup of a great musical partnership. It took me a year to realize they were in love.

—**Paul McCartney**

- I know that women have got it made if they know how to go about it. A woman don't have to work, really, if she don't want to and is smart enough to make a man a good wife, he's gonna take care of her.

—**Dolly Parton**

- We steer completely clear of anything suggestive. We take a lot of care with lyrics because we don't want to offend anybody. The music is the main thing and it's just as easy to write acceptable words.

—**Bill Haley,** 1954

- Punk rock is a bad scene. I don't understand why it has to exist when there's so much in life.
  —Frank Sinatra

- Don't let your mouth write no check your tail can't cash.
  —Bo Diddley

- Keeping up with the times is just a matter of living every day.
  —Judy Collins

- It's not the size of the ship, it's the size of the waves.
  —Little Richard

- If the butterflies in your stomach die, send yellow death announcements to your friends.
  —Yoko Ono

- The finest sensibilities of the age are convulsed with pain. That means a change is at hand.
  —Leonard Cohen

- I try to take fate by the throat, and grab it real hard.
  —Peter Wolf

- When you put six ducks and a rat on stage, the rat's gonna stand out.
  —Grace Slick

- Death is a warm cloak. An old friend. I regard death as something that comes up on a roulette wheel every once in a while.
  —Gram Parsons

- I tried marijuana one time, but it didn't give me anything but a headache.
  —Glen Campbell

- Of course I'm ambitious. What's wrong with that? Otherwise, you sleep all day.
  —Ringo Starr

- I never thought Alice Cooper was ever that hip. Alice was a character and an attitude I created. Alice was always a commodity.
  —Alice Cooper

- The only difference between 'boring' and 'laid back' is one million dollars.
  —Glenn Frey, The Eagles

# Phil Spector: the man behind the Girl Groups

By the end of 1962, Phil Spector had finally reached the point where he felt he was in control of his musical life. He had hit Number 1 with The Crystals' "He's a Rebel," and wrested full ownership of the Philles label away from his partners, Lester Sill and Harry Finfer. Spector was also pleased that he had produced this Number 1 record with session singers as vocalists; it convinced him even more that he could make a hit with whomever he wanted, and that the artists themselves were of secondary importance. Darlene Love, who sang lead, and The Blossoms, who sang backup on "He's a Rebel," were merely paid a session fee. They had no share of the royalties, and they couldn't tour as The Crystals since Spector owned the rights to the name. Lester Sill recalls that when "He's a Rebel" hit the top spot, Philles gave Darlene and her friends a bonus instead of a royalty—"a nice amount...." Darlene Love says the total payment she received for "He's a Rebel" was $1,500.

Phil Spector was an emotional man who would do anything to help out a friend; once you penetrated inside his wall of defenses and he felt secure about the friendship, you were accepted as part of the family. But it often happened that a disagreement or hurt would penetrate the bond, and then Phil would be just as quick to completely cut off the relationship: having no relationship was preferable to having a painful one. The year of 1963 would see Phil establish several important new ties; the pain and the hurt would come later....

Spector's first new hookup came with Darlene Love, an L.A.-based vocalist who had recorded for several years on numerous labels as the lead singer of the vocal trio, The Blossoms. Darlene, born Darlene Wright, also was a much-in-demand session vocalist who sang backup on literally hundreds of records cut in Los Angeles during the early Sixties. Phil was taken not only with her vocal strengths and distinctive sound, but also with the confidence and ease with which she carried them off. After "He's a Rebel," Spector put together a vocal trio of Darlene, Fanita James, another Blossom, and Bobby Sheen, a Clyde McPhatter-type vocalist with whom Phil had previously cut a version of "Zip-A-Dee-Doo-Dah," which sported one of the weirdest guitar solo sounds ever laid down; it took Duane Eddy's echoey twang to the limit. When Phil returned to New York, a major label offered him a $10,000 advance for the master. Spector turned them down, and dubbed the makeshift group Bobby and the Holidays. By the time he issued the record himself on Philles, the group had become Bob B. Soxx and The Blue Jeans, and their innovative reworking of an old standard swept into the Top 10 in January 1963.

The Supremes

As part of his settlement with ex-partners Sill and Finfer, Spector was required to give a portion of the profits from The Crystals' next two releases to the departed duo. The first of these was a Barry Mann-Cynthia Weil tune, "He's Sure the Boy I Love," with Darlene Love once again on lead vocals. The record is drivingly melodic and soulfully visual, cut loose with ragged edges. It's pure rhythm, with pounding drums carrying the beat, maracas and sleigh bells layered on top, and Darlene's vocals exhibiting as honest and heartfelt an emotion as one could ever hope for. Lyrically, the song meshed together topical social images of youthful class values (Cadillacs, unemployment checks, diamond rings, movie stars, etc.), with the belief that true, deep love could rise above these worldly problems and provide real happiness. While others sang of exteriors, "He's Sure the Boy I Love" dug deep into the interiors of both hearts and minds.

The record reached Number 11 on the Top 100, Number 2 on the R&B charts, and then Spector decided that he really didn't want to give any more profits to his former partners. He devised a plan to fulfill his legal obligations and still not pay out one cent in royalties. He went into the studio with the real Crystals and cut a five-minute tune called "(Let's Dance) The Screw." It was a hastily recorded bump-and-grind song with obvious sexual innuendoes, and would clearly, by virtue of its length, music and lyrics, not get played. Spector pressed up some deejay copies, sent them to his distributors, and promptly forgot about the record. "The Screw," allegedly a new dance craze, was merely Phil's big joke; it might have also referred to the fact that Phil was possibly "screwing" his ex-partners out of their potential share of profits. This was the second Crystals record. It sold zero copies; therefore, he would owe Sill and Finfer no money and they would have no further profit participation. As a final touch to the "joke," Spector had his lawyer bellow in a deep voice on the record at various intervals, "Do the screw." Ho-ho-ho—big joke, Phil.

Back in New York scouting around for material, Spector had a meeting set up with fledgling hit-writer Ellie Greenwich: "I was on a first refusal basis with Leiber & Stoller at this point, which meant that I played them all my songs and if they liked them, they could have them; if not, I was free to take them elsewhere. I wrote '(Today I Met) The Boy I'm Gonna Marry,' and Leiber & Stoller weren't too excited by it. I took it to Aaron Schroeder and he liked it and arranged for Phil Spector to hear that and some other songs. So in comes Phil and I'm sitting at the piano playing "It Was Me Yesterday.' Phil was walking around the room fixing his clothes, looking in the mirror and adjusting his hair—all the time making noises while I was playing my song. Finally I said, 'Either you want to hear my songs or you don't.' Phil exploded and stormed out of the room, and everyone in the office felt that Spector was gone for good." A short time later, Phil heard a demo of "The Boy I'm Gonna Marry" and wanted the song, and arranged to meet the writers. "I had a 2 P.M. appointment with Phil and by 2:10 I was ready to leave. But Tony Powers [Ellie's co-writer] convinced me to wait. So we hung around in the hall lobby of 62nd Street and York Avenue until 5:30 or 6:00. I didn't really know who Spector was, or the power he had in the business, and the fact that everybody usually bowed down to him, so when he came I was really mad. 'Hey Phil, if you make an appointment and you can't keep it, you should let us know. You were very rude!' And

I think he just liked the idea that I stood up to him, because we hit it off right away."

Ellie's early songs were written with Tony Powers; Spector wanted a piece of the publishing if he recorded them. When he couldn't get that, he secured one-third of the writer's share and credits, an arrangement that upset Greenwich: "Morally I regret it. I felt that if you wrote a song, you wrote it. I did a lot of editing and putting together of songs for other people, but I never took writer's credits unless I actually wrote it. I passed up a lot of big money deals by refusing to throw in a piece of the action." Spector shared writer's credits on the three Greenwich-Powers songs he recorded, although his input in writing was negligible. After that he became a more active participant in the writing sessions, and was credited and paid accordingly.

In L.A. he cut "Why Do Lovers Break Each Other's Hearts," and "(Today I Met) The Boy I'm Gonna Marry," both featuring Darlene Love. Spector recorded the songs first, and would decide who would be listed as the artist, only after hearing the final product, or even if the record would come out at all. "Why Do Lovers..." became the next release for Bob B. Soxx and The Blue Jeans, and with Bobby Sheen's deep vocals augmenting the bass line, Darlene's voice warmly but strongly selling the message, with saxophones and percussion carrying the rest of the song, the record reached Number 38. "The Boy I'm Gonna Marry" became the first solo release for Darlene Love. It was melodically stronger and more emotionally intense, but a bit slow-paced for AM airwaves. It only reached Number 39. Both these records were special, almost exceptional by 1963 standards, but not *great*—and Spector only wanted to make great records. "If I can't be better than what's around and what's been done before, then what's the point in doing it?" asked Phil. "I'd just rather not make records."

Faced with the fact that his last two releases had barely scraped into the Top 40, Spector decided that he needed a big hit or nothing at all. As an independent record company, Philles would get paid by a series of distributors strung throughout the country. Sometimes payments were slow or nonexistent, and the only real leverage a company had was to hold back a new hit until the distributors paid for the last hit. Spector knew that each record had to be a smash in order to get paid and keep his distributors out there pushing his product — a string of flops could put a small company out of business before it knew what happened. He also felt that he had strayed from his original self-composed commandments: music must be emotional and honest; create a sound on record that no one can copy or cover; and make sure you get paid. He had fought for his control and freedom, and now it was time to put up or shut up. Phil Spector

*The Shangri-Las*

was not about to shut up.

Meanwhile, Ellie Greenwich and her new husband and writing partner Jeff Barry came up with a song which they called "Da Doo Ron Ron," subtitled, "When He Walked Me Home." Spector felt that this was what he was looking for, flew out to L.A. and gathered up his forces. The team included engineer Larry Levine and his Goldstar Studios, arranger Jack Nitzsche, and a slew of session people including some, and sometimes most, of the following: Barney Kessel, Glen Campbell, Billy Strange, Carol Kaye, Irv Rubin, Bill Pitman, and Tommy Tedesco on guitars; Hal Blaine, Earl Palmer, and Ritchie Frost on drums; Leon Russell, Larry Knectal, Harold Battiste, Don Randi, Nino Tempo, Mike Spencer, and Al DeLory on keyboards; Steve Douglas, Jay Migliori, Lou Blackburn, and Roy Caton on horns; Larry Knectal, Jimmy Bond, Ray Pullman, and Wallick Dean on bass; and anyone and everyone on percussion, including Sonny Bono, Frank Kapp, Julius Wechter, Gene Estes, and Nino Tempo. On backup vocals he would use members of various Philles groups as well as Gracia Nitzsche, Jean King, Cher Bono, Edna Wright, and Carolyn Willis. All in all, it was the cream of West Coast session players.

Spector recorded the tracks for "Da Doo Ron Ron" in Los Angeles, but couldn't get the right vocal sound from his West Coast singers, so he flew back to New York and used LaLa Brooks of The Crystals. When he had the whole thing finished, he felt that the record just needed a little more punch and emphasis on the bottom end, but it was already recorded and there were no open tracks available for overdubs. Spector and Larry Levine came up with an ingenious solution: while they were mixing "Da Doo Ron Ron" down to the mono master, Spector had Nino Tempo out in the studio playing a bass drum with mallets for accents wherever needed. As the original tracks were mixed into mono, they also added in Nino Tempo's live drum figures. Anyone looking today to find Tempo's drums on the original three tracks just won't find it—it only exists on the mono master, and that's it.

"Da Doo Ron Ron" itself was everything Spector wanted: it thunderously blares out from the opening, with drums, handclaps, and saxophones mixed together into what would soon become known as "the wall of sound." The vocals, melody and story line are exhilarating; Tempo's drum overdub is stunning in its power and definition; and the whole thing is over before you can catch your breath. It's a record that exudes a life of its own and demands not only attention, but almost a total immersion into its driving, exuberant vitality. It was a huge hit both on the pop and R&B charts, and also was the first record to make the Spector sound popular around the world. Phil followed this up with "Then He Kissed Me," which took the popular Latin *baion* beat uptempo at a galloping pace, and added lush, swirling strings over the top. Once again, it was a global smash.

The Crystals themselves were busy touring, but their dissatisfaction with Spector was growing each day. For one, they were unhappy about Phil's usage of Darlene Love as vocalist on so-called Crystals records. They also felt that they should be earning more money from record royalties. They also feared for their future and wanted to branch out in other musical directions and develop a night-club act, sing more middle-of-the-road fare and perform some songs with a jazz flavor to them. In the studio, they would sit for hours while Spector worked on the sound and arrangements of the musicians. He would listen to the tracks endlessly at ear-piercing volume, and ignore their boredom or their needs. He would make them sing over and over again—leads, backgrounds, even individual sections. They would record songs that would never be released, and their request for input on choice of material fell on deaf ears. They believed that Spector was egomaniacal and was making their records so noisy and murky that they couldn't cut through the din. Spector told an interviewer at the time, "The cloudier and fuzzier a record is, the more honesty and guts it has." The conflicting views of Spector and The Crystals were poles apart and not getting any closer.

The original quintet of Crystals was now down to a foursome, as Mary Thomas dropped out and Pat Wright was replaced with Frances Collins. It was this quartet that made the first trip to England in early 1964, headlining an extensive and successful six-week tour with Johnny Kidd, Joe

*The Shirelles*

Brown, Heinz and Manfred Mann. Manfred Mann actually backed up The Crystals on their live dates, coming as close as five musicians could to approximating the Spector recorded sound. The members of Manfred Mann also took The Crystals down to a series of small rock clubs in London, where the girls mixed with the new British rock groups, all of whom loved The Crystals' records and respected the Spector sound. After a six-week tour without one day off, the girls were set to relax, sightsee, and shop around London, but they suddenly got a call from Spector in New York who told them to take the next plane home for a recording session. The Crystals, along with tour manager Arthur Pemberton, did so but were not happy about it.

Although The Crystals were coming off two Top 5 hits in a row, Spector's eccentricities and disregard for their needs frayed their nerves. They wanted out. Phil refused and made their records even noisier than before. The first was "Little Boy," a recording that had some of the sound but none of the vitality or emotional impact of The Crystals' previous hits. It only reached Number 92. Then came "All Grown Up," which was loosely based on an old Chuck Berry song, and this one didn't even crack the Top 100. In England, Spector pulled "Little Boy" off the market and issued "I Wonder," an adventurous track which didn't quite come together and lost the vocals somewhere in a swirling pit of background fuzz. To top it off, Spector was lavishing most of his time and effort on recording a new female vocal group for Philles, The Ronettes, and The Crystals were considerably less than a priority. They ultimately bought their way out of their contract with Spector and went over to United Artists for a handful of releases, none of which ever made the charts. The Crystals had become one of the most popular and recognizable recording artists of their era, but with the massively solid foundation of Phil Spector's input pulled out from under them, they were buried by the wall of sound that now lay crumbled at their feet.

Back in Los Angeles, things were not going so well between Spector and his vocal star Darlene Love either. Some of Darlene's complaints were similar to those of The Crystals, but a prime disagreement between Phil and Darlene arose out of Spector's insistence that Darlene curtail her outside career work. Darlene occasionally did make public appearances with Bob B. Soxx and The Blue Jeans, as well as doing solo spots of her own, but these were exceptions to the rule. Darlene was happier and more financially secure singing on record dates in Los Angeles, and backing big-name singers on their live shows. On top of the fact that these commitments often led to scheduling conflicts with Spector sessions, Phil was incensed that Darlene continued to make records for other labels with The Blossoms, and even did solo records under pseudonyms. In

1964, The Blossoms sang behind several artists in the popular movie *The T.A.M.I. Show*, and then they began to appear weekly on the national TV show, *Shindig*. Here, they not only backed up most of the artists on the show, but they also had regular on-camera song spots of their own. (Many of Spector's regular session musicians played each week on *Shindig* as well: their television payments were significantly higher than their recording studio work earned.) Jack Good, producer of *Shindig*, said at the time, "These three girls [The Blossoms] are quite remarkable. They back approximately ten numbers per show, but they don't have to be taught the songs. You tell them what they will be singing, and that's it. The number is polished and ready for the first run-through. They are individually great, and as a group, sensational."

Darlene Love was one of the few Philles artists who was outspoken in her opinions with Phil. She might not have been happy with material or financial arrangements, and as time went by she became increasingly irritated by lengthy sessions where she would give her all, and then records would never get released. Spector, for one reason or another, just didn't feel they were good enough, commercial enough, or right for the moment. On the other hand, Phil was still irked by Darlene's continuing non-Spector related work. They managed to patch up their differences and decided to create a hit with a song called "Stumble and Fall." First issued in the fall of 1964, the record was quite marvelous and seemed almost guaranteed to bring Darlene back into the Top 30 and maybe much higher, but then things fell apart. Darlene remembers, "We made this record to hit where the other ones had flopped. It had been out for about two weeks, and then Phil and I got mad at each other and he pulled it back off the market by sending out a note to the radio stations saying that the pressing plant had inadvertently put out the wrong record, and that there would be another one very soon." Others close to the scene felt that a major factor in the withdrawal of the record was that Spector's last few singles had been relatively unsuccessful, and that the initial reaction to "Stumble and Fall" was less than enthusiastic. (When Spector pulled the record back, he rushed out The Ronettes' "Walking in the Rain" in its place, and that *was* a major hit.) Whatever the reason, the result was that Darlene was mad at Phil, and Phil was mad with Darlene. They split, and never made another Philles record together. First The Crystals and now Darlene Love had left the fold, but Spector was busily immersed in a series of records with a group with whom he felt the closest emotional ties. The records and the group would come to be recognized and remembered as the pinnacle of the girl-group era. The records were many.

The group was The Ronettes.

# ROCK ON FILM

### ABBA THE MOVIE (1977)
Visual record of ABBA's Australian tour, with fictional subplot of reporter trying to secure an interview with the Swedish stars. Even though ABBA is often billed as "the most popular group in the world," this film has had only limited distribution in the U.S. Included are some of their marshmallow-rock classics such as "Dancing Queen," "The Name of the Game," and "S.O.S."

### ALICE'S RESTAURANT (1969) [Arlo Guthrie, Pat Quinn]
A hippie commune and restaurant serves as a haven for draft-evader Guthrie in this episodic Sixties serio-comedy. Arlo's famed talking blues, "Alice's Restaurant Massacre" is better when heard on record than *seen* in this dramatic reenactment. Film features use of a Joni Mitchell composition, "Song to Aging Children," in a touching scene which takes place in a graveyard.

### AMERICAN GRAFFITI (1973) [Ron Howard, Richard Dreyfuss, Cindy Williams, Harrison Ford, Suzanne Somers, Candy Clark and others]
Twenty-four hours in the lives of a group of California small-town teenagers in the film that (though set in the Sixties) almost singlehandedly invented Fifties rock and roll nostalgia. If George Stevens had directed a beach party movie, it might have looked something like this. Rock fills the air from beginning to end in this semi-classic that helped bring youth flicks to a new respectable plateau. Among the sounds spun by DJ Wolfman Jack are such inarguable classics as "Why Do Fools Fall in Love?" by Frankie Lymon and the Teenagers, "Little Darlin'" by the Diamonds, Fats Domino's "Ain't That a Shame," and Chuck Berry's "Johnny B. Goode." Other well-known numbers heard include "Green Onions," "The Stroll," "Teen Angel," "Get a Job," "To the Aisle," "All Summer Long," "Since I Don't Have You," and "Do You Wanna Dance?" Note: When the film was re-released in 1979, certain sequences, originally cut due to the insistence of Universal's top brass, were put back in by director Lucas, so great was his clout after the success of *Star Wars*.

### AMERICAN HOT WAX (1978) [Tim McIntire, Laraine Newman]
Robert Altman-esque week in the life of pioneer rock DJ Alan Freed. Cheerful, if somewhat over-reverential, overview of rock's beginnings recycles the shared plotline of all those Fifties musicals about irate town fathers and mothers trying to shut down rock and roll. The myth of Freed (and rock) endlessly reflects back and

forth in an infinite hall of mirrors to extremely satisfying results! Sparked by Jerry Lee Lewis thrashing out "Whole Lotta Shakin' Goin' On" and "Great Balls of Fire," Chuck Berry duck-walking and wailing his way through "Reelin' and Rockin'" and Screamin' Jay Hawkins howling out "I Put a Spell on You," all in a specially staged live concert sequence. Atmospheric soundtrack music by Jackie Wilson, Buddy Holly, The Drifters, The Moonglows, The Cadillacs, The Turbans, The Spaniels, The Elegants and The Zodiacs.

## AMERICAN POP (1981)

Animation used to tell the story of four generations of an American family and the music they (and by extension the entire nation) were involved with. Though the musical eras portrayed run all the way from vaudeville to new wave, the film concentrates heavily on contemporary sounds. Some of those used in conjunction with Bakshi's none-too-impressive rotoscope animation techniques include: Pat Benatar's "Hell Is for Children," Fabian's "Turn Me Loose," The Doors' "People Are Strange" and Big Brother's "Summertime." The final blowout production number is done to Bob Seger's "Night Moves" — the dubious implication being that this song represents the alpha and omega of American Pop to date. (An okay song, but music of the spheres it's not!)

## AMERICATHON (1979) [Harvey Korman, John Ritter]

The time is the near future (1998); the U.S. is broke and the President (Ritter) hosts a national telethon to keep the country from going under. Feeble satire based on an idea by two members (Proctor and Bergman) of The Firesign Theatre. Eddie Money sings "Get a Move On" and "Open Up Your Heart," Elvis Costello does "(I Don't Want To Go to) Chelsea" and "Crawlin' to New York." The Beach Boys and Nick Lowe heard on soundtrack.

## BEACH BLANKET BINGO (1965) [Frankie Avalon, Annette Funicello, Buster Keaton & others]

More of the same amiable nonsense, fourth in the AIP "beach" series. This time, "Dee Dee" (Annette Funicello) is distraught when "Frankie" falls for another girl, "Sugar Kane," played by TV's Linda Evans. The usual musical hired hands in these frolics, Dick Dale and the Del Tones, replaced here by The Hondells. The "Dee Dee"/"Frankie" solos and duets ("I Think These Are the Good Times," etc.) are as uninspired as ever.

"American Hot Wax"

### BEACH PARTY (1963) [Frankie Avalon, Annette Funicello]

"Frankie's" (Avalon) plans for a moonlight beach tryst with "Dee Dee" (Annette Funicello) get sidetracked when she invites the whole gang along. So he retaliates by faking an affair with a beach vamp, played by Eva Six. Biker "Eric Von Zipper" (Harvey Lembeck) pops up to wreak havoc every so often, and all the while a sympathetic anthropologist (Bob Cummings) hovers around the edges of the activity taking notes on teen tribalism in this true slice of pop-art Americana. Don't blink or you'll miss Beach Boy Brian Wilson standing around in the background as an extra in this, the first of AIP's fabulously successful "beach" series. The nearly non-stop farcical fun only pauses long enough for an occasional sappy solo or duet by Funicello and/or Avalon, but the music revs up again when Dick Dale and The Del Tones turn on their tangy surfin' beat. Songs by Roger Christian and Gary Usher include: "Surfin' and Swingin'" and "Treat Him Nicely."

### BEAT STREET (1984)

The second and better of the films to come out that featured rap singing, breakdancing and street kids, Harry Belafonte produced this tale of Bronx kids hoping to make it. Non-stop music and dance. Music by Grandmaster Melle Mel and The Furious Five.

### BEATLEMANIA (1981) [Mitch Weissman, Tom Teely, David Leon, Ralph Castelli]

Film of long-running stage show featuring four young musicians dressed up to look like The Beatles singing the songs the Fab Four made famous in as-near-to-identical-sound-style as possible, occasionally interrupted by slides and film clips of Sixties era events. Not our cup of tea, but for some people, imitations like this are the next best thing to actually being there. Songs include "Twist and Shout," "She Loves You," "Strawberry Fields Forever," "A Day in the Life," "Helter Skelter," "With a Little Help from My Friends," "Penny Lane," "Revolution," "Let It Be," "The Long and Winding Road" and other Beatles hits.

### BIG TNT SHOW, THE (1966) [The Byrds, Joan Baez, The Lovin' Spoonful, Ike & Tina Turner, Ray Charles, Donovan, etc.]

This concert film arrived hard on the heels of, and is similar to, the very successful *TAMI Show*. Just like that film, *TNT* was filmed with the "Electronovision" process, and before it was released was slated to be called *The TAMI Show II*. Two music personalities of note not listed in the official credits appear in *TNT*, for at one point producer Phil Spector can be seen accompanying (of all people!) Joan Baez on the piano; and at another, when Petula Clark reaches out to touch the hand of an adoring fan it turns out to be none other than a young (pre-Seeds) Sky Saxon (again, of all people!). Filmed in 1965 at Los Angeles's Moulin Rouge night club, while *TNT* lacks the impressive talent lineup of *TAMI*, it is still recommended viewing. Performances of note: The Ronettes singing "Be My Baby," Ray Charles doing "Georgia on My Mind," The Byrds with "Tambourine Man," Clark's "Downtown" and a manic Bo Diddley's "Hey, Bo Diddley."

### BIKINI BEACH (1964) [Frankie Avalon, Annette Funicello]

Two Frankie Avalons for the price of one are offered in this lightly entertaining entry in the "beach party" series. The singer-actor appears as both the regular

"Frankie" character and a Beatle-wigged Britisher called "Potato Bug." Keenan Wynn appears as a real-estate speculator who wants to take over the surf crowd's playground in a subplot. This musical is primarily devoted to kidding the American teenager's infatuation with things English. Little Stevie Wonder lets loose with "Fingertips" in the finale.

### BLACKBOARD JUNGLE, THE (1955) [Glenn Ford, Vic Morrow, Sidney Poitier]

Glenn Ford portrays a school teach, "Dadier," who's unprepared for the caged animals he meets up with at his new assignment at a blighted New York City school. The high school toughs taunt him (they call him "Daddy-O") and rape and pillage left and right in this grim portrait of the failure of the American educational system. If it weren't for this film, you might not be reading this book right now. The bold (for 1955) and successful use of Bill Haley's recording of "Rock Around the Clock" on the soundtrack made *Blackboard Jungle* the official first-ever rock-and-roll movie. *Apres Haley, le deluge!*

### BLUE HAWAII (1961) [Elvis Presley, Joan Blackmore, Angela Lansbury, Jenny Maxwell]

Elvis in a musical drama/comedy about a poor little rich boy who yearns for a simple life, without the influence of his domineering mother. Playing the part of the son of a wealthy pineapple plantation owner, Elvis spends most of his screen time horizontal and supine in a film marking the beginning of a thirteen-year cinematic decline from which he never fully recovered. The tepid songs, which form a large part of the problem here, include: " The Hawaiian Wedding Song," "Ku-U-I-Po," "Beach Boy Blues" and "Ito Eats."

### BLUE SUEDE SHOES (1979) [Bill Haley, Ray Campi, Freddie "Fingers" Lee]

Filmed record of the first Rock-and-Roll Weekend at England's Great Yarmouth Holiday Camp. Leather clad unreconstructed rockers and their pony-tailed girlfriends look on at the music-making of simpler and more fun-filled kinds of rock by Ray Campi and Matchbox, and Freddie "Fingers" Lee. Also included is coverage of a 1978 London concert by Bill Haley and His Comets as they zip through enthusiastically received replays of "Rock Around the Clock" and "Shake, Rattle and Roll." Some vintage clips of Gene Vincent, Eddie Cochran and several other first-wave rockers are also thrown in for good measure.

### BLUES BROTHERS, THE (1980) [John Belushi, Dan Aykroyd]

"Jake" (Belushi) and "Elwood" (Aykroyd), The Blues Brothers, are sprung from the pokey, and waste no time getting back into musical action. The only question is, does the music scene want them back? $30,000,000 worth of car chases and wrecked property are sunk into the oldest plot in the movie musical business — raising money for an orphanage by putting on a show. Belushi and Aykroyd's besuited and sunglassed "hipsters" weren't terribly funny on *Saturday Night Live* (or at least a little went a long way) and they were even less so here. Aretha Franklin's roof-raising version of "Think" almost single handedly manages to turn this bloated sub-Abbott and Costello programmer around, but the racist tendencies of this backhanded tribute to rhythm-and-blues undoes the well-intentioned work of Aretha, Ray Charles ("Shake a Tail Feather"), James Brown ("The Old

Landmark") and Cab Calloway ("Minnie the Moocher"). Booker T. and Steve Cropper also appear as supporting musicians, but Sam and Dave, on whom The Blues Brothers' act is based, are conspicuous by their absence. The excellent musical direction is by Ira Newborn.

*Aretha Franklin, "The Blues Brothers"*

### BOB MARLEY AND THE WAILERS LIVE! (1978)
Concert film sponsored by Marley's record label, Island, captures the singer/musician and his band in performance at a 1977 London concert. Although somewhat wearing on the eyes, *Wailers Live!* probably represents the best extant footage of the late reggae mega-star Marley. Songs include "Trenchtown Rock," "I Shot the Sheriff," "Lively Up Yourself," "Running Away," "No More Trouble," "Exodus" and "The Heathen."

### BORN TO BOOGIE (1972) [Marc Bolan, T-Rex, Ringo Starr]
Documentary about T-Rex also includes concert footage and staged sequences, i.e., a mad tea party take-off. Ringo's directorial work here remindful of touches he used in *Magical Mystery Tour*. A musical highlight is Mark Bolan and the band's working over their hit, "Bang a Gong." Other songs include: "Children of the Revolution," "Cosmic Dancer" and "Tutti-Frutti."

### BREAKIN' (1984)
First film to be released that featured the breakdancing craze. Young girl is introduced to street dancing by two top breakers. They win the big break dance contest after expected trials and tribulations and are offered film opportunity as a result. Music by Gary Remel and Michael Boyd.

**BUDDY HOLLY STORY, THE (1978)** [Gary Busey, Don Stroud]

Film of the life of early rock great Buddy Holly. This throwback to the year of Universal Pictures' musical biopics of the Fifties (e.g., *The Glenn Miller Story*, etc.) takes massive liberties in re-telling the life of the rockabilly king, Holly. Richie Valens and The Big Bopper are portrayed, but nowhere in sight is Holly mentor, Norman Petty. But Gary Busey (doing all his own singing) scores on the dramatic level in an Oscar-nominated performance. Music includes nearly all the Holly hits including: "That'll Be the Day," "Peggy Sue," "Rave On," "Maybe Baby," and "It's So Easy." Musical director: Joe Renzetti.

**BYE BYE BIRDIE (1963)** [Dick Van Dyke, Ann-Margret, Bobby Rydell]

When an Elvis-like rocker pays a visit before his induction into the army, havoc is raised in a small town by both its oldsters and (especially) its youngsters. Presley-mania was already past its peak (and The Beatles were waiting in the wings) when Hollywood turned out this version of the hit Broadway musical. The film was a launching vehicle for Ann-Margret, whose diminutive milquetoast boyfriend is played by Philly rocker, Bobby Rydell. Jessie Pearson bumps and grinds like Al Capp's "Stupifyin' Jones" in the Presley-esque part of "Conrad Birdie."

**CAVEMAN (1980)** [Ringo Starr, Barbara Bach, Dennis Quaid, John Matuszak]

Misfit caveman "Atouk" (Ringo) leaves the tribe of the bullying "Tonga" (Matuszak) and sets up his own prehistoric society. Ringo and his friends' discovery of music through an impromptu stone-age jam session is a highlight of this wonderful *Alley Oop*-like comedy. Music by Lalo Schifrin.

**CHARLIE IS MY DARLNG (1965)** [The Rolling Stones]

Documentary of The Rolling Stones' 1965 two-day tour of Ireland. Interviews with fans and The Stones themselves take up much of the film's running time, with only a brief amount of footage used for "live" performance, with versions of "This Could Be the Last Time" and "It's Alright." The band is also viewed backstage, jamming on an old music hall ditty, "Maybe It's Because I'm a Londoner." While the group incessantly gets in and out of limos, and on and off stage, their actions are accompanied on the soundtrack by sounds from many of their recordings, including: "Get Off of My Cloud," "Heart of Stone," "Satisfaction" and "Goin' Home." Additionally, there is a score based on Stones songs by Mike Leander.

**CONCERT FOR BANGLADESH (1972)** [George Harrison, Bob Dylan, Eric Clapton, Ravi Shankar, Ringo Starr, Leon Russell, Badfinger, Klaus Voorman, Billy Preston]

Film of one of the major media events of 1971, a benefit concert at New York's Madison Square Garden (planned by Harrison) for the starving nation of Bangladesh. Highlights include Harrison's "Bangladesh" and Dylan's singing of "Blowin' in the Wind." Also seen and heard: "Something" (Harrison), "It Don't Come Easy" (Ringo Starr), "Just Like a Woman" (Dylan). Recording supervision by Phil Spector.

**CREAM'S FAREWELL CONCERT (1968)**

Just what you'd think this film is, from its straightforward title — a record of the group's very last concert ever, performed in 1968 at London's Royal Albert Hall.

Musical highlights: "Spoonful," "Politician," "I'm So Glad" and lots of others of the best-selling songs by this early proto-supergroup (Jack Bruce, Ginger Baker and Eric Clapton). Note: 52m. and 40m. versions of this film, a.k.a. *Cream's Last Concert*, also are in circulation.

### DANCE CRAZE (1980) [Bad Manners, Bodysnatchers, The English Beat, Madness, The Selector, The Specials]

Ska music is not quite reggae, and just this side of rock and roll — somewhere in between, actually, and this performance film is the first feature to be devoted exclusively to 1980's practitioners of this Jamaican-inspired hybrid sound. Most of the bands are young, British *and* racially integrated, and the music they make here is as infectious as it is offbeat. The visual quality of this ska *TAMI Show*, however, leaves much to be desired. The Specials do "Concrete Jungle," "Man at C and A," and "Nite Club;" The Selector shanks out on "Three Minute Hero" and "Missing Words" and The English Beat reprise their hit, "Mirror in the Bathroom."

### DECLINE ... OF WESTERN CIVILIZATION, THE (1980) ["X," Alice Bag Band, Black Flag, Catholic Discipline, Circle Jerks, Fear, Germs]

What do "X" do in their spare time? What kind of pets did the late Darby Crash keep? Do punk runkers put their pants on one leg at a time, just as you and I, or are they lowered into them? All these questions, and more, are answered in this excellent made-for-mass (well, almost) consumption collection of interviews and performances with/by some of L.A.'s premier punk bands. Music: "White Minority," "Revenge" (Black Flag); "Manimal" (Germs/Darby Crash); "Underground Babylon" (Catholic Discipline); "Beyond and Back," "Johnny Hit and Run Pauline," "We're Desperate" (X), and much more by "Bags," "Jerks" and Fear.

### DIVINE MADNESS (1980) [Bette Midler, The Harlettes]

Elaborately staged docu of Bette Midler's 1979 concerts in Pasadena, Ca. Bette has gone way beyond being just another capable clown princess, and it shows in this appealing film. While the divine Miss M. may not be everyone's idea of a rock singer, her excellent concert film can teach a thing or two to all rockers with a yen for the leap to the big screen. Songs include: "Paradise," "Boogie Woogie Bugle Boy," "Big Noise from Winnetka" and "Shiver Me Timbers."

### D.O.A. (1980) [The Sex Pistols, Iggy Pop, The Clash, The Dead Boys, Stiv Baters, Rich Kids, X-Ray Specs, Generation X, Sham '69, Augustus Palo, Terry & the Idiots]

Extensive coverage of The Sex Pistols' seven-city U.S. tour combines with film of other groups and interviews for an overview of the international punk scene, circa 1978. Some critics heaped scorn on this music documentary when it opened. We feel, however, that the film's messiness and scattergun approach tends to complement its subject matter, punk rock music. With mechanical regularity, *D.O.A.* shifts away from The Sex Pistols to interview fans, and zeros in on the music of groups that followed in the wake of The Pistols, like The Clash and The Dead Boys. Also seen are several poignant segments featuring Terry and the Idiots — a motley London band inspired by The Sex Pistols who are shown playing in a pub and throwing in the towel, after literally being spat upon exactly *once*. Most fascinating, however, is what one might call *The Sid and Nancy show*, an extremely intimate and intense film of terminally wasted Pistol Sid Vicious and his nearly as far gone girlfriend, Nancy Spungen, being interviewed in a hotel room. Writers used to trot out adjectives like "harrowing" for this sort of Sid/Nancy thing, and it seems to fit most aptly here. (Spungen and Vicious died shortly thereafter.) The Sex Pistols are seen on their whistle-stop tour doing "Anarchy in the U.K.," "God Save the Queen," "Pretty Vacant" and several others. Iggy Pop, although listed in the cast, is only *heard* singing "Nightclubbing," and X-Ray Specs (Spex) sing "Oh Bondage, Up Yours" on screen.

### DON'T KNOCK THE ROCK (1956) [Bill Haley & His Comets, Alan Freed, Alan Dale]

A riot breaks out at a rock-and-roll dance and although the music played there by Bill Haley wasn't *really* to blame, town elders place a ban on "the new sound" — until DJ Alan Freed convinces all concerned that rock is but "a harmless outlet for today's youth." Who says that sequels are never up to the originals? This film is even more inspired than the movie that started it all, *Rock Around the Clock*. It tackles head-on such controversial and burning issues of the day as "suggestive dancing," heavy petting, payola and teen-age curfews. Haley and His Comets are on hand again from *Clock* (doing the title tune, "Calling All Comets," "Rip It Up" and others); but the *real* rock-and-roll here is courtesy of Little Richard, on display with "Tutti Frutti" and "Long Tall Sally."

### DOUBLE TROUBLE (1967) [Elvis Presley, John Williams, Norman Rossington, Chips Rafferty, Annette Day, Yvonne Romain]

A singer (Elvis Presley) saves an heiress (Annette Day) from a series of mysterious threats on her life. Threats can't stop Elvis from warbling the likes of "Long-Legged Girl," "Could I Fall in Love," "Blue River" and the title tune in this standard operational Presley musical.

### EASY RIDER (1969) [Peter Fonda, Dennis Hopper, Jack Nicholson, Luke Askew, Phil Spector, Toni Basil, Karen Black]

Two hippies (Peter Fonda and Dennis Hopper) polish off a cocaine deal, then take off on their motorcycles for the New Orleans Mardi Gras. Along the way, they meet up with an alcoholic Southern lawyer (Nicholson). Eventually, the three of them are murdered by rednecks. One of the most well-received films (critically *and* financially) ever pitched to the youth market — so much so that attendance for it went way beyond the original targeted audience. *Easy Rider* was the film phenom of its year, opening the floodgates for a spate of youth-oriented films. Fonda and Hopper's Kerouac-inspired travels are counterpointed by soundtrack rock including "The Pusher," and "Born To Be Wild" (Steppenwolf), "Wasn't Born to Follow" (The Byrds), "The Weight" (The Band) and "Ballad of Easy Rider" (Roger McGuinn).

### ELVIS — THAT'S THE WAY IT IS (1970) [Elvis Presley, The Sweet Inspirations]

By the time this documentary on Elvis was made, his career was in a definite downswing. He was still the king, alright, but his recordings weren't selling nearly as well as they did before and his film activity was bottoming out. This movie was but one part of a several-pronged attempt to bring the star's popularity level back up to its former state. This, then, is a permanent record of Elvis's so-called "Vegas comeback." Here we have, to use Lenny Bruce's phrase, "show business heaven" personified, as we see Elvis strut his stuff not only before the fascinated eyes of the likes of Cary Grant, Sammy Davis, Jr. and (!) Xavier Cugat, but also of average Joes like you 'n' me. Twenty-seven songs are featured, including "That's All Right Mama," "Can't Help Falling in Love with You," "Suspicious Minds," "Blue Suede Shoes," "Heartbreak Hotel" and "Mystery Train."

### *ERIC CLAPTON AND HIS ROLLING HOTEL (1980)* [Eric Clapton, Muddy Waters, Elton John, George Harrison]

Film of a 1979 German tour by Eric Clapton and musical company. "The Rolling Hotel" of the film's title is a luxury train built by the Third Reich's Goering, and it serves as the transportation for Clapton and crew on their German blitz. Muddy Waters was also along for the ride and can be seen singing "Got My Mojo Working" and "Mannish Boy." Clapton does "Layla," "Lay Down Sally," "Tulsa Time" and others, and is joined for one of his concert encores by George Harrison and Elton John.

### *FAME (1980)* [Irene Cara, Berry Miller, Paul McCrane, Linda Clifford, Laura Dean]

Episodic musical/drama of four years in the life of a group of students at New York's High School for the Performing Arts. If you're wondering whatever happened to Lesley ("It's My Party") Gore, she's alive and well and writing songs for the likes of this update of the old MGM Mickey-Judy musicals. Several hit songs by Michael and Lesley Gore and Dean Pitchford (including "Hot Lunch Jam," "Out Here on My Own," "Red Light" and the title tune) all originated from this film/soundtrack album package.

### *FILLMORE (1972)* [Grateful Dead, Jefferson Airplane, Santana, Hot Tuna, Boz Scaggs, and others]

Concert film of the last days of San Francisco's Fillmore West rock emporium, interleaved with entrepreneur Bill Graham's reminiscences of the heyday of the S.F. "scene." Not all the groups listed in the credits are seen with complete versions of songs, but those who do include: Santana ("In a Silent Way"), The Grateful Dead ("Casey Jones"), Jefferson Airplane ("We Can Be Together") and Cold Blood ("You Got Me Humming").

### *FLASHDANCE (1983)*

Enormously successful, trend-setting film proving rock music and flashdancing could draw large audiences without stars and without convincing plot. Alex (Jennifer Beal) is a welder in Pittsburgh steel mills by day, a club dancer at night, and is being pursued by her handsome boss (Michael Nouri). Great dance sequences were actually performed by the uncredited Marine Jahan. Grammy-award-winning single, "What a Feeling" sung by Irene Cara. Also featured Michael Sembello's "Maniac" and Laura Branigan's "Imagination."

### *FLAMING STAR (1960)* [Elvis Presley, Barbara Eden, Delores Del Rio]

Elvis plays a half-breed Indian torn between his native American culture and the white man's in this almost music-less Presley film. Only the title song is heard in Don Siegel's sincere, but confused, try to change the pace for singer Presley.

*Elvis Presley*

### FOOTLOOSE (1984)

Was actually in production ahead of the ground-breaking film *Flashdance*, but released afterward. It looked to capture the same audience of filmgoers, weaned on MTV – satisfied by minimal plot, lots of dance and rock music. Kevin Bacon played "Ren," a young student who has moved from Chicago to a small, mid-western town where popular music and dance have been outlawed by the local pastor (and father of Ren's love interest). Ren wins the town over, the dance is held and the big production number, "Footloose" is the result. Songs from the hit album: "Footloose," "Let's Hear It for the Boy," "Holding Out for a Hero," sung by Bonnie Tyler, "Almost Paradise," sung by Mike Kerio and Ann Wilson.

### FOLLOW THAT DREAM (1963) [Elvis Presley, Anne Helm]

Or, *The Lauderdale Hillbillies* as Elvis and his family belligerently homestead on valuable Florida real estate in this standard Presley comedy-musical. Elvis sings the title tune, "What a Wonderful Life," "I'm Not the Marryin' Kind" and several others.

### FRANKIE AND JOHNNY (1966) [Elvis Presley, Nancy Kovak-Mehta]

Period riverboat setting for Presley musical based on the old barroom ballad – only this time out, F&J live happily ever after. Film represents a temporary up-swing over most Elvis movie vehicles from around this time. Songs include the title tune, "Come Along" and "Petunia."

### FUN IN ACAPULCO (1963) [Elvis Presley, Ursula Andress]

Elvis plays a singer/lifeguard enamored of femmatador Ursula Andress in this hands-across-the-border project. Elvis' films had been banned in Mexico for several years after showings of *G.I. Blues* caused riots; and this shot-on-location musical signalled rapprochement and a lifting of the ban. Among the songs: *"El Toro,"* "Marguerita," "The Bullfighter Was A Lady," and the title tune.

### G.I. BLUES (1960) [Elvis Presley, Juliet Prowse]

Elvis is a singing G.I. chosen by his mates as their candidate in a race to see who can get a date with the notoriously undatable Juliet Prowse. When Elvis was drafted in 1958 many felt the time away from his fans would kill his career. Colonel Parker, however, gambled all by imposing a total recording blackout for the two years the singer was away. It worked! *G.I. Blues*, Elvis' first post-service film, was almost as major a movie event as his first movie, *Love Me Tender*. This re-launch vehicle plays around with much of the myth surrounding Private Elvis Presley, but a de-mystification process is in operation here, for unlike before, he portrays someone not larger than life, but only a guy who *just happens* to be able to sing. *The New York Times*' film critic, Bosley Crowther, wrote of Elvis's return film, "gone is the wiggle, the lecherous leer, the swagger, the unruly hair, the droopy eyelids and the hillbilly manner of speech." Lest you think this was criticism on the writer's part, it was not! It was *praise*. Elvis *did* seem less threatening here, and *G.I. Blues'* hitless musical package ("Wooden Heart," "Pocketful of Rainbows," "Big Boots," etc.) was another sign that a downill movie slide had begun.

### GIMME SHELTER (1971) [The Rolling Stones, Ike & Tina Turner, The Jefferson Airplane]

Documentary of the notorious 1969 Stones concert at Altamont, California. Most everybody, of course, remembers the real life snuffout climax, but what is often forgotten is how much good, well-filmed footage of The Rolling Stones is contained in this film—especially the early Madison Square Garden portion. It's ironic that these self-styled priests of anarchy should be so totally at a loss when confronted by the real thing, the crowd at Altamont. Aside from the moral issues revolving around actually showing the murder, this is a manual for cliché-avoidance in rock filmmaking. Tina Turner is seen doing a spectacular version of "I've Been Loving You Too Long," and songs by The Stones include: "Jumpin' Jack Flash," "Satisfaction," "You Gotta Move," "Wild Horses," "Brown Sugar" and (while the much-publicized killing is taking place just a few dozen yards away) "Sympathy for the Devil."

### GIRL CAN'T HELP IT, THE (1956) [Jayne Mansfield, Tom Ewell, Edmund O'Brien]

Jayne Mansfield, Tom Ewell, Edmund O'Brien, Fats Domino, Gene Vincent and The Blue Caps, The Platters, Little Richard, Eddie Fontaine, Eddie Cochran. O'Brien plays a gangster who can't bear the thought that his girlfriend (Mansfield) is a "nobody," so he hires press agent Ewell to turn her into an overnight superstar. In true screen fashion, Ewell and Mansfield flip over each other and before its happily-ever-after fadeout, this delirious comedy presents some of the best-looking rock-and-roll ever (before or since) on a movie screen. Mansfield, here, is a succulent A-bomb just waiting to explode (with rock music as the detonator) in this satire of record industry hucksterism—and the 1950's in general. The performers on hand, among them Fats Domino, Little Richard and Gene Vincent, constitute a virtual master class on how to rock and roll. And the look of the film is just right! Not like the earlier black-and-white rock musicals, but with Cinemascope, stereophonic sound and Technicolor you can eat with a spoon. Mansfield, playing a talentless would-be singer, was the ultimate Fifties sexual commodity and the aura she exuded works in perfect complement to the hit-and-run 2.32 sec. foreplay-to-orgasm viscerality of the (then) "new sound." Music includes: the title tune and "She's Got It" (Little Richard), "Blue Monday" (Domino), "Be Bop A Lula" (Vincent) and "Twenty Flight Rock" (Cochran).

### GIRL HAPPY (1965) [Elvis Presley, Shelley Fabares]

Elvis plays a girls' college chaperone in this frothy musical whose numbers include: "Do the Clam" (bet you thought that was from *Clambake*), "Spring Fever," "Ft. Lauderdale Chamber of Commerce," and "She's Evil."

### GIRL ON A MOTORCYCLE (1968) [Marianne Faithfull, Alain Delon, Tetragrammaton]

A gone-straight housewife (Faithfull) just can't hack her new way of life and reverts to her former wild lifestyle and lover (Delon). Wonderful unmitigated trash.

Picture this: Pop icon, Marianne Faithfull, swaddled in black leather from head to toe, roars toward the camera astride a chopper. She screeches to a halt. Cut to next shot. Faithfull excitedly rushes into a room, exhorting Delon (no mean icon himself) to "SKIN ME!" If this whets your appetite, they're ninety beautifully photographed minutes more in this movie whose title, in some markets, was changed to the rather blunt one of *Naked Under Leather*. Score by Les Reed.

### GIRL'S TOWN (1959) [Mamie Van Doren, Mel Tormé, The Platters, Paul Anka]

Van Doren plays a good/bad girl who gets hit with a bum murder rap and is sent to a prison run by some kind of "nuns." There, she experiences some *sotto* (and not so *sotto*) "lez" stuff, and so terrified is she by her ordeal that she nearly "gets religion." *Variety* said, "Scenes of Miss Van Doren in the tightest of costumes exchanging badinage with nuns are in dubious taste, to say the least." Anka plays a singer whose big numbers in the film are "Lonely Boy" and "Ave Maria," and while Mamie serves time, The Platters keep time to "Wish It Were Me" in this *klassic* which also bears the yummy alternate title of *The Innocent and the Damned*.

### GO GO MANIA (ORIG. POP GEAR) (1965) [The Animals, The Beatles, Herman's Hermits, The Spencer Davis Group, The Nashville Teens, Billy J. Kramer and the Dakotas, Peter and Gordon, The Honeycombs]

A mock concert film, i.e., shot on stark, brightly lit sets, with lip syncing and dubbed-in audience shrieks and applause. Top Brit rock jock, Jimmmy Saville (bearing a remarkable resemblance to comic Marty Feldman), does the emcee honors as most of the acts go through the motions to one or two of their hit records. The one exception is The Beatles, who are seen in good quality color newsreels doing "Twist and Shout" and "She Loves You." For a while it's fun to watch, but after a time even the most ardent of British Invasion fans will probably begin to twitch. Performances include: "House of the Rising Sun," "Don't Let Me Be Misunderstood" (The Animals), "World Without Love" (Peter and Gordon), "Little Children" (Billy J. Kramer) and "I'm into Something Good" (Herman's Hermits). Note: Go-Go Mania's cinematographer was the late Geoffrey Unsworth, whose more distinguished credits include: *2001*, *Tess*, *Superman* and *Murder on the Orient Express*.

### GRATEFUL DEAD MOVIE, THE (1977) [The Grateful Dead]

More a gathering of the tribe than mere concert movie, this over-two-hour affair captures The Dead at a five night 1974 San Francisco stand, running down a few dozen of their more popular anthems — the introduction of each one being met with knowing and adoring frenzy by the crowds on hand. A long, dazzling animation sequence by Gary Guiterez opens the film.

### GREASE (1978) [John Travolta, Olivia Newton-John, Jeff Conaway, Stockard Channing, Frankie Avalon, Sha-Na-Na]

Most of the harmless clichés about teen life in the Fifties are trotted out in this homage to that era, as seen through the eyes of on-again-off-again romantic duo "Danny" (Travolta) and "Sandy" (Newton-John). On the Broadway stage, this long-running cartoonish replay of "the way it was" was a thin but tolerable entertainment, harmless Fifties rock-and-roll revisionism. But *Grease*, the movie, tends to get pulled out of shape in a distorted effort to make the doo-wop past at one with the disco present. Original music by Jim Jacobs and Warren Casey ("You're the One That I Want," "Beauty School Dropout" and "Look at Me I'm Sandra Dee," etc.). The title tune, written especially for the film by Barry Gibb, is sung on the soundtrack by Frankie Valli. Grease contains extensive use of vintage atmosphere-inducing songs as "Hound Dog," "Tears on My Pillow" (Sha-Na-Na) and "Love Is a Many Splendored Thing." Also heard, Cindy Bullens and Louis St. Louis.

## GREASE II (1982)

Proof that sequels are risky business, Grease II attempted to match its predecessor in offering motorcycle gang, beautiful girl, sexy guy and Sixties rock music. Maxwell Caulfield as the English guy failed to light up the screen. Michelle Pfeiffer fared better, but couldn't save the day. Broadway/rock score by Louis St. Louis.

## GREAT ROCK AND ROLL SWINDLE, THE (1980) [Malcolm McLaren, Nancy Spungen, The Black Arabs and Jerzimy]

The anti-Beatles,The Sex Pistols, in the dark side of A Hard Day's Night, i.e., a heavily fantastical version of how The Pistols came to pass. Originally the group's premier film éffort was supposed to be a vehicle entitled (with Russ Meyer set to direct) Who Killed Bambi? Then, it is said, Johnny Rotten balked, and Sid Vicious was arrested for killing his girlfriend Nancy Spungen. Then Vicious died, and both the project and group fell apart. The Svengali and manager of these punk innovators, Malcom McLaren, was undaunted, however, and so he set about concocting this fictional docu-cartoon of How It All Began, using scraps left over from the aborted film, together with any footage of The Sex Pistols he could lay his hands on, plus animated material also done for Bambi. Because of this — McLaren's undisguised hucksterism — Swindle turns out to be one of the most honest rock films of them all. Songs include "God Save the Queen," "Anarchy in the U.K.," "No Feelings," "Pretty Vacant," "Holiday in the Sun" (Sid's hilarious version of "My Way"), and "Johnny B. Goode" — or bits and pieces thereof. Note: In an unprecedented move, British censors forced the distributors of the film to add (not delete as per usual) footage with moralistic title cards heavy-handedly pointing out the deaths of Sid Vicious and Nancy Spungen.

## HAIR (1979) [John Savage, Treat Williams, Nicholas Ray, Beverly D'Angelo, Annie Golden]

Screen adaptation of the famed Broadway "tribal love-rock musical," with the big hits from the original ("Let the Sun Shine In," "The Age of Aquarius," "Black Boys/White Boys," etc.) blasting forth from the screen in teeth-rattling Dolby sound. Lyrics by Gerome Ragni and James Rado. Music by Galt MacDermot.

## HARD DAY'S NIGHT, A (1964) [The Beatles]

The Beatles (playing themselves) make a TV variety show appearance, but the broadcast is complicated by both their adoring hysterical fans and Paul's "grandfather" (Wilfred Brambell), whose tart tongue keeps getting the boys into scrapes. Ringo, encouraged by granddad, wanders off for a "lark" just before the schedule TV show. But in the nick of time the Beatles' drummer is found and everything

*The Beatles, "A Hard Day's Night"*

*Jimmy Cliff,
"The Harder They Come"*

goes as planned—to the relief of a much-harried TV director. Not much of a plot, but the success of The Beatles' film debut caught nearly everyone by surprise for its deliverance of the rock musical from the bondage of exploitation to the realm of "serious" entertainment and even (dare we say it?) Art. Richard Lester's antic direction and Alun Owen's witty script combined to make this film not only a topflight musical, but one of the most important films of the Sixties as well. Original songs composed for the film include "I'm Happy Just To Dance with You," "And I Love Her," "If I Fell," "Tell Me Why," "Can't Buy Me Love" and the title tune. "She Loves You," "I Wanna Hold Your Hand," "I Should Have Known Better" and "Any Time at All" are also heard. When the film was re-released in 1981 a song not included in the original—The Beatles singing "I'll Cry Instead" over a montage of photos—was added to the opening of the film.

### *HARDER THEY COME, THE (1972)* [Jimmy Cliff, Carl Bradshaw]

Tragic tale of musician (Cliff) who comes to Kingston, Jamaica from the outlands, only to become, briefly, a recording star and an unwitting political martyr. The "Third World" implications of this extraordinary work are inescapable by the time Cliff is gunned down by the villains. If regular-hour moviegoers didn't know a good thing when they saw it, a more adventuresome crowd did, for this Jamaican feature was one of the first weekend midnight movie hits. Cliff portrays a purist reggae star concerned with protecting his country's music from commercial exploitation—in what amounts to nearly a tract for Jamaican nationalism, i.e., the pop star as cultural guerilla. Soundtrack album from the film is, perhaps, the essential reggae album. Cliff sings "You Can Get It If You Really Want," "Many Rivers To Cross," "Sitting in Limbo," and the title tune, with additional atmospheric use of music by The Maytals, The Melodians, The Slickers, Desmond Dekker and Scotty.

### *HARUM SCARUM (1965)* [Elvis Presley, Fran Jeffries]

American pop star "Johnny Tyronne" (Presley) is abducted to the country of "Lunarkand" while on tour in the Middle East and swept up into political intrigue. All ends well, however, as he eventually resurfaces hale and hearty in, where else? Las Vegas. By this point Elvis was (bump 'n') grinding films out at the rate of *exactly* three per year. And it shows! Dozens of extras running around in jalabas and Frederick's of Hollywood leftovers in what appears to be L.A.'s Griffith Park, a poor substitute for the film's alleged Mid-East locations. The brains behind this seven day wonder? None other than producer Sam (*Rock Around the Clock*) Katzman. Songs include: "Harem Holiday" (the film's British title), "Golden Coins," "My Desert Serenade" and "Kismet."

### *HEAD (1968)* [Frank Zappa, The Monkees, Annette Funicello, Timothy Carey, Sonny Liston, Teri Garr, Jack Nicholson and Bob Rafelson]

A day in the life of the self-confessed "plastic pop group" The Monkees. Created for television to capitalize on the appeal of The Beatles, The Monkees had a number of Top 10 hits and (for awhile) a teenybopper following. Their popularity, however, was fast fading by the time this film—their $8\frac{1}{2}$, as it were—reached the screen. Six new songs are shoe-horned in between parody vignettes (Maria Montez movies, *Golden Boy*), pseudo-surrealistic segments (a romp through Victor Mature's hair), clips from old movies (*Dracula, Gilda*) and stock footage.

Musical numbers include "Porpoise Song" (by Carole King and Gerry Goffin), "As We Go Along" (by Carole King and Toni Stern), "Daddy's Song" (by Nilsson), and "Can You Dig It" (by Peter Tork).

## HEAVY METAL (1982)

Animated cartoon feature based on the "adult" comic strip of the same name, consists of five loosely connected episodes all of which revolve around extra-terrestrials fighting for control of a magically powered secret substance. It was William Burroughs in *Naked Lunch* who first used the scientific term "heavy metal" as part of "hip" argot, replacing "too much," "out of sight" and the like. He probably never suspected it would eventually come to stand for a strain of hard rock music—not to mention the laser-gun carrying ample breasted women of this big screen "head" fantasy. Background sounds provided by such "heavy metal" exponents as Blue Oyster Cult ("Veterans of the Psychic Wars"), Black Sabbath ("Mob Rule"), Nazareth ("Crazy?"), Trust ("Prefabricated"), Grand Funk Railroad ("Queen Bee") and Sammy Hagar (the title tune).

*The Beatles, "Help"*

## HELP! (1965) [The Beatles, Leo McKern, Eleanor Bron, Victor Spinetti]

The Beatles' second film finds them again playing themselves and here they are pursued by members of an Eastern religious cult (led by Bron and McKern), a crazy scientist (Spinetti) and his bumbling assistant, all of whom are after a magically-endowed ring that has inadvertently come into the lads' possession. Director Lester, who shepherded The Beatles through their first film effort, *A Hard Day's Night*, for their second lets all the famed "Lesterian" touches get a trifle out of hand—so much so that at times the real stars of the film appear to be the bigger budget and Technicolor camera, not The Beatles. But it's still plenty of fun, and The Beatles continue to shine in this shaggy dog tale about zealots who'll stop at nothing to remove the ring from Richard Starkey's finger. Songs: "Help," "Night Before," "You've Got To Hide Your Love Away," "Ticket To Ride," "I Need You," "You're Gonna Lose That Girl" and "Another Girl." Score by George Martin.

***I WANNA HOLD YOUR HAND (1978)*** [Nancy Allen, Bobby Di Cicco, Marc McClure, Susan Kendall Newman, Murray the K]
Four teenagers attempt to crash a Beatles TV performance, with the ensuing events and interactions altering, irreversibly, the courses of their lives. This film from the team of Zemeckis and Gale (*1941, Used Cars*) isn't about The Beatles *per se*, but the phenomenon of Beatlemania, and as such it is a loving momento of a week's-worth of madness in the life of New York City—those few zany days when almost none of its inhabitants could escape even the most minuscule detail of the Great British Invasion. Liberal use of all early Beatles hits on soundtrack, including: "I Wanna Hold Your Hand," "Please Please Me," "I Saw Her Standing There," "Love Me Do" and thirteen others.

***IMAGINE (1972)*** [John Lennon, Yoko Ono, George Harrison, Phil Spector, Dick Cavett]
Performances of various Lennon and Ono compositions ("Imagine," "Crippled Inside," "Jealous Guy," "Power to the People," "Oh My Love" and others) interspersed with home movies, TV clips and collage. Also appearing on screen are such diverse celebrities as filmmaker Jonas Mekas, Fred Astaire and Jack Palance. Most of the music comes from either John's *Imagine* or Yoko's *Fly* albums.

***IT'S YOUR THING (1970)*** [The Isley Brothers, Patti Austin, Moms Mabley, Ike and Tina Turner, Brooklyn Bridge, Clara Ward]
The Isley Brothers produced, and appear in, this film of an all-star soul show held in 1969 at New York's Yankee Stadium.

***JAILHOUSE ROCK (1957)*** [Elvis Presley, Judy Tyler]
Elvis (unfairly) spends time in the slammer on manslaughter charges. After he is sprung, he becomes a Presley-like singing sensation, thanks to the help of his manager (Tyler) with whom he gradually becomes romantically involved. One of the great iconographic moments in rock film history is Elvis' cootch dance to the title song — in an otherwise routine show-biz soaper. (Although the film stands head-and-shoulders above mid- and late-period Elvis movie fare.) Nothing else is quite up to that dazzling production number, but looking his dangerous and surly best, Elvis does get off a few good lines like "Honey, it's just the beast in me," and he sings five fine songs: "Jailhouse Rock," "I Want To Be Free," "Baby I Don't Care" (all written by Jerry Leiber and Mike Stoller), "Don't Leave Me Now," and "Young and Beautiful." Brief on-screen appearance by Stoller.

***JAMBOREE (1957)*** [Kay Medford, Paul Carr, Freda Holloway, Jerry Lee Lewis, Fats Domino, Carl Perkins, Frankie Avalon, Lewis Lymon and the Teenchords, Slim Whitman, Count Basie]
Love duo and recording stars "Honey" and "Pete" spat and reconcile over and again as they rocket their way up the record charts. Lots of rock stars on hand, but the music they make only adds up to a handful of minutes in this heavily-plotted tale of retrograde teen stars. (They're kind of a road show Debbie and Eddie.) "Honey" (whose singing voice is ghosted by Connie Francis) and "Pete" solo and duet on what seems like five dozen songs. Most of the music is perfunctorily staged, but there is one memorable segment of Jerry Lee Lewis singing "Great Balls of Fire" that looks for all the world as if it were photographed by someone

who knew what he was doing. Other music includes; "Wait and See" (Domino), "Cool Baby" (Gracie), "I'm Glad All Over" (Perkins), "Don't Wanna Be Teacher's Pet" (Avalon) and "Hula Love" (Knox).

### JANIS (1975) [Janis Joplin, The Kozmic Blues Band, Big Brother and the Holding Company, The Full Tilt Boogie Band]

Documentary on the life and hard times of major rock force Janis Joplin. Excerpts from Monterey Pop and Woodstock, as well as concert performances in Frankfurt, Calgary and Toronto are on display here, as well as some moving material on Janis, her freak flag flying, visiting her tenth high school reunion in Port Arthur, Texas. Also included is an excerpt from a touching TV interview with Dick Cavett. Although interest in Joplin has remained great even since her death, this Canadian-made venture came and went very quickly when it opened in 1975. Songs include: "Ball and Chain," "Tell Mama," "Kozmic Blues," "Cry Baby," and "Move Over."

### JAZZ SINGER, THE (1980)

Remake of the Jolson classic in a vanity production starring Neil Diamond with Sir Laurence Olivier as his aging father, the temple cantor. The son wants to break with religious tradition and sing rock 'n' roll. Goes to LA to make it in rock and meets up with Lucie Arnaz, who helps his career. Reconciliation with father brings film mercifully to an end. Soundtrack album fared better than film and included: "Love on the Rocks," "Hello Again," "Acapulco" and "You Baby."

### JIMI HENDRIX (1973) [Jimi Hendrix]

Interviews with family, friends and an old army superior of Hendrix, plus familiar footage of the guitarist mixed with some previously unshown musical material, and a rather-much-of-a-downer Hendrix/Dick Cavett TV interview all are seen in this assembled tribute to Jimi. Glimpsed briefly in various contexts and surroundings are such musicians as Little Richard, Lou Reed, Mick Jagger, Eric Clapton and Pete Townshend. All the various assemblings of The Experience and the Band of Gypsies (Cox, Miles, Mitchell & Redding) perform in whole (or in part): "Red House," "Machine Gun," "Johnny B. Goode," "In from the Storm," "Rock Me Baby," "Hey Baby," "Like a Rolling Stone," "Purple Haze," and (from Woodstock) "The Star-Spangled Banner."

### KID GALAHAD (1962) [Elvis Presley, Lola Albright]

Semi-musical remake of old Warner Brothers boxing drama finds Elvis portraying a reluctant championship fighter. During time-outs Kid Presley works his way through several musical numbers including: "King of the Whole Wide World," "This Is Living," "Riding the Rainbow," and "I Got Lucky."

### KIDS ARE ALRIGHT, THE (1979) [The Who]

Immensely satisfying compilation film of The Who's career. Old promo films, recent concert material, ancient concert footage, TV interviews and variety show appearances all heaved up on the screen in seemingly random fashion (with occasional quasi-narrational assist from Ringo Starr) — and yet, despite this lack of a scheme, or perhaps because of it, this scattergun effort is one of the better and more useful theatrical rock-and-roll films of recent years. See what appears to be a thousand guitars destroyed. *Hear* The Who doing new versions of most of their biggest selling recordings. *See* Keith Moon apparently go all to pieces on nationwide British TV—in this docu-overview of four of the most influential rock 'n rollers of all time. Songs include: "Summertime Blues," a Tommy medley, "My Generation," "A Quick One," (from the unreleased Stones film *Rock-and-Roll Circus*), "Won't Get Fooled Again" and "Who Are You?"

### *KIDS ARE UNITED, THE (1980)* [The Jam, Ultravox, The Pirates]
Straight-ahead docu of 1978 Reading (England) Rock Festival features a standout set by The Jam.

### *KING CREOLE (1958)* [Elvis Presley, Carolyn Jones, Walter Matthau]
Elvis is a night club singer who gets involved with some shady characters in yet another in a long line of movies he made about the show business school of hard knocks—and thanks to director Michael Curtiz it all hangs together nicely. This is Elvis' last film before he entered the service, and after he returned to civilian life he rarely made another film even as good as this one. Elvis sings five Lieber/Stoller songs: "Crawfish," "You're the Cutest," "Let Me Be Your Lover Boy," "Danny Is My Name," the title tune, plus eight others.

### *KISSIN' COUSINS (1964)* [Elvis Presley, Yvonne Craig]
Elvis as twins! He plays both an Air Force lieutenant and down-home country boy in this featherweight musical about the government's foiled attempts to build a missile site on some choice backwoods property. The Elvises sing "There's Gold in the Mountains" and "Smokey Mountain Boy."

### *LADIES AND GENTLEMEN, THE ROLLING STONES (1974)* [The Rolling Stones]
Musical documentary of The Stones' 1972 U.S. tour. Most unusual for a presentation of this sort, there are no interviews with the band, or fans, no behind-the-scenes poking and prodding by the cameras—just straight-ahead music, in a film that was lavishly presented in quadrophonic sound, at "hard ticket" prices. The Stones were lucky to have a slick concert film of their U.S.A. swing in reserve to counteract the bad publicity that surrounded their off-stage activities at the time. This record of their on-stage triumphs is a far cry from the sinister frolics captured by Robert Frank in his *Cocksucker Blues*, shot at the same time. The band slashes through fourteen uninterrupted numbers including: "Brown Sugar," "Bitch," "Gimme Shelter," "Tumblin' Dice," "Love in Vain," "Midnight Rambler," "Street Fightin' Man," and "Jumpin' Jack Flash."

### *LADY SINGS THE BLUES (1972)* [Diana Ross, Billy Dee Williams, Richard Pryor]
Singer Billie Holiday's rise from ghetto backstreets to jazz stardom is complicated by drug addiction and romantic problems. While this elaborate musical drama has little to do with the actual facts of the great singer's life, Diana Ross' performance rings true, as does her singing. Wisely, she doesn't try to imitate the Holiday sound, but instead works at capturing the flavor of "big band" vocal styling of the Forties. Songs include "God Bless the Child," "Good Morning Heartache," "Strange Fruit" and "My Man." Other music by Michel Legrand.

***LAST WALTZ, THE (1978)*** [The Band, Bob Dylan, Joni Mitchell, Neil Diamond, Emmylou Harris, Neil Young, Van Morrison, Ron Wood, Muddy Waters, Eric Clapton, The Staple Singers, Ringo Starr, Dr. John]

Documents The Band's (Robertson, Danko, Manuel, Hudson and Helm) Thanksgiving Day, 1976, farewell-as-a-group concert at San Francisco's Winterland. Other musicians on hand for the occasion represent a veritable cross-section of a quarter century of pop and rock-and-roll—from Waters to Butterfield, Dylan to Diamond, Morrison to Mitchell, etc. While the bulk of the film was shot at Winterland, the most stunning sequences (The Band, Harris, The Staples) were photographed on an MGM sound stage. Hands down, the most meticulously crafted concert film ever made. Director Scorsese left nothing to chance as he choreographed and storyboarded almost every musical sequence in the film in advance, down to the last detail. The end results more than justified all this fussiness in this beautifully made concert film. Songs include: "Cripple Creek," "Stagefright," "The Night They Drove Old Dixie Down," "The Weight" (The Band); "Helpless" (Young); "Mannish Boy" (Waters); "Coyote" (Mitchell), "Baby Let Me Follow You Down," "I Shall Be Released" (Dylan, The Band, Starr and Wood) and "Mystery Train" (Butterfield).

***LET IT BE (1970)*** [The Beatles, Billy Preston]

Rehearsals and recording sessions for The Beatles' *Let It Be* album, plus an impromptu concert on the roof of the Abbey Road studios are the focus of this docu filmed only slightly before the group split up. The internal friction the band was experiencing when the film was made is obvious, with tension between George and Paul being especially noticeable. All the while the inscrutable Yoko Ono sits off to one side of the musical action, taking it all in expressionlessly. The mood only lightens during the latter half of the film, when the boys go up on the roof for some mid-day serenading to a crowd that rapidly assembles down in the streets. One minute into the concert and pandemonium sets in for blocks around — traffic stops, businessmen begin climbing over rooftops, etc. Songs include: "Don't Let Me Down," "Maxwell's Silver Hammer," "I've Got a Feeling," "Across the Universe," "I Me Mine," "The Long and Winding Road," "Shake, Rattle and Roll," "Kansas City," "Get Back" and "Let It Be."

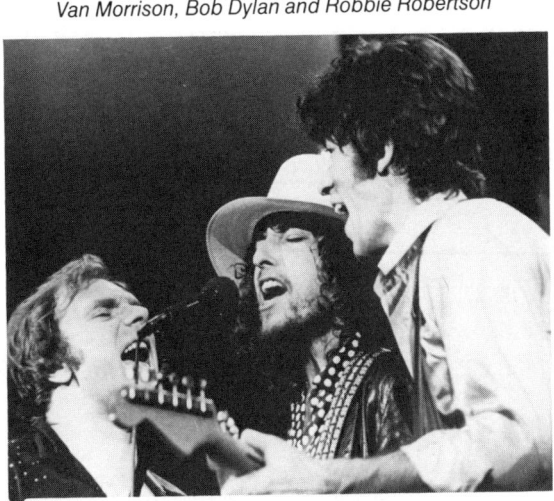

*Van Morrison, Bob Dylan and Robbie Robertson*

***LET THE GOOD TIMES ROLL (1973)*** [Little Richard, Fats Domino, Chuck Berry, The Shirelles, The Five Satins, Bill Haley and His Comets, The Coasters, Danny and the Juniors, Chubby Checker]

A lively and largely successful try at doing something a little different with the concert film format. Colorful record of Richard Nader's rock revival shows mixes in newsreels of Fifties fads and fashions, and through split-screen, juxtaposes old and new footage of various vintage rock stars running through "live" medleys of their classic recordings in front of widely receptive crowds.

***LET'S ROCK (1958)*** [Julius LaRosa, Phyllis Newman, Paul Anka, Danny and The Juniors, The Royal Teens, Roy Hamilton]

A Forties-style balladeer (LaRosa) finds his fame rapidly bottoming out, until he gets wise and hops on the rock and roll bandwagon. Helping to awaken the rock consciousness of LaRosa's washed-up crooner are Paul Anka (singing "I'll Be Waiting for You"), the Royal Teens (with "Short Shorts") and Danny and the Juniors (with their classic "At the Hop").

***LOVE ME TENDER (1956)*** [Elvis Presley, Richard Egan, Debra Paget]

Confederate soldier (Egan) leads a band of men in robbing the U.S. mint (just as the Civil War concludes); meanwhile, back on the farm, his kid brother (Elvis) has just married the fiancée (Paget) of the presumed-dead Egan. Both plot strands, then, combine for a fittingly smashing climax. The biggest movie debut ever!—Elvis!—and practically the greatest film sensation since Jolson talked. *LMT* hasn't aged particularly well, but it's light years beyond some of the later Elvis films like *Clambake*. In what's supposed to be the Civil War era, Presley anachronistically bumps and grinds his way through four songs: "Poor Boy," "We're Gonna Move," "Let Me" and the title tune.

***MAGICAL MYSTERY TOUR (1967)*** [The Beatles]

Largely improvised film chronicles the adventures of The Beatles and friends as they take a ride on the *MMT* bus. One can guess why American TV execs refused to air this (at a time when The Beatles couldn't have been hotter) after previewing it. What was expected must've been a straightforward all-singing, all-dancing variety show, but what The Beatles delivered was a personal and thoughtful statement. Because of the surrealistic nightmarishness of some of *MMT*'s scenes, the film is occasionally disturbing, but overall it is most charming in spite of its fragmented, herky-jerky mildly pretentious style. The songs written for, and visualized in, this rock *Un Chien Andalou* include: "I Am the Walrus," "Fool on the Hill" and the title tune.

***MAHOGANY (1975)*** [Diana Ross, Billy Dee Williams]

The rise and *rise* of a superstar designer/fashion model, "Mahogany" (Ross) is the focus of this trash maven's delight. So Diana Ross wants to do a moldy old Lana Turner-style fantasy! So what?! She's entitled! This enormously entertaining piece of Swiss cheese features Diana (heard) singing "Do You Know Where You're Going To?" Also on the soundtrack are, among others, The Temptations and Jermaine Jackson. Motown magnate Berry Gordy replaced original director Tony Richardson part way through the filming. Score by Michael Masser.

### MAN WHO FELL TO EARTH, THE (1976) [David Bowie, Rip Torn]

A visitor from a drought stricken planet (Bowie) comes to Earth and establishes an international electronics corporation to finance aid for his world. Gradually, he is undone by U.S. corporate interests and his own emotional weaknesses. The cinematic answer to the old Bowie musical question, "Is there life on Mars?" Well, yes there is, and Bowie's it in this William Burroughs-ian sci-fi affair. While "the man who sold the world" doesn't sing here, he does manage to exploit all the mythical material of his songs in this fragmented narrative package based on Walter Tevis' novel. Critically well-received, still this film never managed to achieve much box office momentum when first released. Now, though, it is steadily played on the movie revival house circuit. Original music by Papa John Phillips and Stomu Yamashta. Also soundtrack usage of recordings by Roy Orbison ("Blue Bayou"), the Kingston Trio and many other non-rock artists like Artie Shaw and Louis Armstrong. Note: A truncated version of this film, less 20 minutes, was in release in the U.S. until 1981, at which time Roeg's original was put into circulation.

### MISTER ROCK AND ROLL (1957) [Alan Freed, Teddy Randazo, Chuck Berry, Little Richard, The Moonglows, Frankie Lymon]

DJ Freed in the title role sets out to prove the preposterous premise to concerned citizens that rock and roll isn't responsible for juvenile delinquency. His *aides-de-camp* include Chuck Berry, who sings "Oh Baby Doll" and Little Richard, who gets the kids all riled up with "Lucille" and "Keep A Knockin'." Lots of music, little plot in this telethon-like quickie.

### MONTEREY POP (1968) [Jimi Hendrix, Otis Redding, Jefferson Airplane, Janis Joplin and Big Brother and the Holding Company, Country Joe and the Fish, The Mamas and the Papas, The Animals, Canned Heat, Simon and Garfunkel, Booker T. and the M.G.'s, Ravi Shankar, The Who]

The Big pre-Woodstock breakthrough concert film. In spite of some of the film's visual pretensions, there are still more than enough great performances to put this filmed record of the 1967 Monterey International Pop Festival over the top. Highlights include The Who ("My Generation") and Jimi ("Wild Thing") – both neck-and-neck in the amp-smashing sweepstakes, Janis ("Combination of the Two," "Ball and Chain") and Otis ("I've Been Loving You Too Long"). Other music includes: the Jefferson Airplane doing "Today" and Eric Burdon and The Animals singing "Paint It Black." The optical distortion of Redding almost beyond recognition is a typical example of the film's visual failings, but still in all, *Monterey Pop* is required viewing.

### MORE AMERICAN GRAFFITI (1979)

Sequel to the 1973 film, attempted to pick up the lives of the original characters beginning two years later. Each scene was accompanied by its own song. Most of the original cast reassembled for the sequel including Ron Howard, Candy Clark, Bo Hopkins, Paul Le Mat, MacKenzie Phillips, Cindy Williams. Richard Dreyfuss was the exception. Like the original, film featured a look at life in America through these characters' lives – including Viet Nam war, rioting and protest (war footage is shown with The Supremes' "Stop in the Name of Love" on the soundtrack).

***NATIONAL LAMPOON'S ANIMAL HOUSE (1978)*** [John Belushi, Tim Matheson, John Vernon, Donald Sutherland]

The most financially successful comedy ever made, this rowdy free-for-all details the frat house rivalry between super-straight "Omega House" and wild-and-crazy "Delta" at the mythical "Faber College." While most of this is fun, some scenes are in very questionable taste—especially one in which the kids visit an all-black night spot. There's rock-and-roll running through most of the action, "Louie Louie" by the Kingsmen, functioning as "The Delts" personal anthem. Other songs heard include "Shout" by The Isley Brothers, "Twistin' the Night Away" by Sam Cooke, and "Tossin' and Turnin'" by Bobby Lewis. John Belushi tears his way into the R&B classic "Money" during a party scene. Non-rock music by Elmer Bernstein. Song "Animal House" written and performed by Stephen Bishop.

***NO NUKES (1980)*** [The Doobie Brothers, Jackson Browne, Gil-Scott Heron, Crosby, Stills, Nash & Young, James Taylor, Carly Simon, Jessie Colin Young, Bruce Springsteen, John Hall, Bonnie Raitt, Niocolette Larsen]

The above-listed stars (as well as many others not in this film) pooled their talents for a 1980 pro-solar, anti-nuclear benefit at New York's Madison Square Garden. This is a filmed record of that well-intentioned but, ultimately, rather enervated parade of socially conscious rockers. Highlights include: "The Times They Are A Changin'," "Mockingbird" (Taylor and Simon); "Runaway" (Raitt); "Teach Your Children," "Long Time Gone" (CSN&Y); "Lotta Love" (Doobies, Larsen); "Before the Deluge" (Browne); "Get Together" (Young); and "Stay," "Devil with the Blue Dress On" (Springsteen).

***ONE-TRICK PONY (1980)*** [Paul Simon, Marc Winningham, Lou Reed, The B-52's, The Lovin' Spoonful, Sam and Dave, Tiny Tim]

Simon plays a rock musician whose popularity has diminished considerably but who, to the detriment of both his marriage and his sense of personal worth, keeps trying to rekindle his career. Sixties superstars never faded even halfway to Eighties oblivion, the way Simon's "Jonah" does in this semi-autobio(?). And it's hard to swallow the idea of songs like "Late in the Evening" being deemed passée in the film, whereas in real life those same tunes are Top 10 hits. But even though Simon the screenwriter is annoying, Simon the actor is often charming. To help things along there's an appearance by rocker Lou Reed as a record producer and on-screen appearances by The B-52's ("Rock Lobster"), Sam and Dave ("Soul Man"), The Lovin' Spoonful ("Do You Believe in Magic?").

***PERFORMANCE (1970)*** [Mick Jagger, James Fox, Anita Pallenberg, Michele Breton]

"Chas" (Fox), a petty hoodlum on the lam from gangsters he betrayed, takes refuge in the mansion of retired pop star, "Turner" (Jagger). Chas's experience while dwelling in this "decadent" parallel universe constitute the main action in this hypnotic film. When the Warner Brothers brass first viewed this seminal cult classic, their reaction was said to have been apoplectic. With its fragmented narrative, extremes of sex and violence, drug-induced hallucinations and arcane literary references, *Performance* is clearly a film designed to disturb. Underneath its Borgesian surface and bisexuality, however, lies a simple gangster-on-the-run-meets-intellectual-outcast story straight out of *The Petrified Forest*. All Cam-

Prince

mell, Roeg and company did was flesh it out in contemporary rock terms. In the Leslie Howard role, Jagger disarms the viewer as easily as he charms the slick teddy boy portrayed by Fox. But even the sociopathic hood Bogie played in *The Petrified Forest* would have been thrown off balance by rock recluse (*Sunset Boulevard* by way of Oscar Wilde) Turner.

### PURPLE RAIN (1984)
Including the soundtrack written, composed and performed by 24-year-old Prince Rogers Nelson. Critics and the public have given much acclaim to the film *Purple Rain*. The film features Prince as "the Kid," a promising young rocker in the Minneapolis rock scene. The product of a mixed marriage, "the Kid" must overcome family turmoil between his musically frustrated father (Clarence Williams III) and his mother (Olga Karlatos) who becomes a punching bag for the father's frustration. "The Kid" retreats into his own musical creativity. The film is said to be based on Prince's life. His energetic performances should not be missed. Supporting roles include Apollonia Kotero (leading lady) of Apollonia 6; Morris Day, once a drummer for Prince, now in his own band The Time, and The Revolution. The *Purple Rain* soundtrack and movie simultaneously hit Number 1 on the charts within a few weeks of their July 1984 release. Number 1 song "When Doves Cry" and "Let's Go Crazy" are included.

### QUADROPHENIA (1979) [Phil Daniels, Leslie Ash, Garry Cooper]
Period Sixties tale of mods and rockers in England — and specifically of one deeply anguished mod (Daniels), whose alienation, fueled by drugs, finally ends

in self-destruction. Near-perfect integration of rock and story. Film is based on The Who's 1973 album of the same name, and very effectively utilizes Who sounds, as well as atmospheric, evocative oldies by James Brown, The Kingsmen, The Ronettes, The Crystals, The Cascades and Booker T. and the M.G.'s. Soundtrack songs by The Who (executive producers of the film) include: "5:15," "I Am the Sea," "Love Reign Over Me" and "I Am the One." Note: Daniels is leader of rock group The Cross, and Sting, of The Police, appears in brief dramatic role.

**ROCK AROUND THE CLOCK (1956)** [Bill Haley and His Comets, Alan Dale, Alan Freed, The Platters, Freddie Bell and His Bellboys, Ernie Freeman]

"I like your sound," a city slicker (Dale) tells Haley when he stumbles upon the singer and his band (The Comets) wailing away at a small town sock hop. Dale likes it so much, in fact, that he helps launch Haley and his new "sound" (rock-and-roll) into the big time. Somewhere along the line, influential DJ Freed (as himself) steps into the picture. And the rest is (rock-and-roll) history! This first-of-its-kind movie was an international box office bonanza. When Katzman's competition saw what the producer had wrought (and just about every studio in town) jumped on the bandwagon to rush rock "product" into release. Katzman, though, understood the teen market better than just about anyone else, and over the next few years the veteran producer assumed the position of past-master of the rock musicals sweepstakes. Haley and his group zip through nine of their early big hits (the title tune, "Rudy's Rock," "Rock," "Mambo Rock," "Rock-a-Beatin' Boogie," "Happy Baby," "See You Later, Alligator," "Razzle Dazzle" and "ABC Boogie"), and midway through the film The Platters step in to harmonize on two of their big sides, "Only You" and "The Great Pretender."

**ROCK, ROCK, ROCK (1957)** [Alan Freed, Tuesday Weld, Teddy Randazzo, Frankie Lymon and the Teenagers, La Vern Baker, Chuck Berry, The Flamingos, The Moonglows, Johnny Burnette, The Three Chuckles]

Teenager Weld suffers the torments of first love against the background of Alan Freed leading various rock acts in and out of the picture. In her movie debut, Weld's voice is dubbed by Connie Francis. Berry sings "You Can't Catch Me," Lymon does "I'm Not a Juvenile Delinquent" and Baker works out on her hit "Tra La La."

**ROCKY HORROR PICTURE SHOW, THE (1975)** [Tim Curry, Susan Sarandon, Barry Bostwick, Richard O'Brien, Jonathan Adams, Little Nell, Pat Quinn, Meat Loaf]

When their car breaks down in a rainstorm, newlyweds "Brad" and "Janet" seek shelter in the mansion of "Dr. Frank N. Furter," self-described "sweet transvestite from transexual Transylvania." Numerous seductions and musical numbers ensue. This engaging rock-and-roll send-up of horror films began as a camp for homosexuals, but by now it's become something of a rite-of-passage for precocious teenyboppers. Entering its second half-decade (with no signs of losing steam) of weekend midnight screenings at over 200 U.S. theaters, Rocky Horror has turned into the "counter-culture's" answer to *The Fantasticks*. To say that the showings are accompanied by "audience participation" would be the understatement of all time. Songs by Richard O'Brien include "Science-Fiction Double Feature," "Sweet Transvestite," "Toucha Toucha Touch Me" and "The Time Warp."

***ROCK 'N' ROLL HIGH SCHOOL (1979)*** [P.J. Soles, Vincent Van Patten, Mary Woronov, Paul Bartel, The Ramones]

A *Hard Day's Night* meets Jean Vigo's *Zero for Conduct* as the students of "Vince Lombardi High" stop at nothing to see their idols, The Ramones, in person -- in spite of opposition from "Principal Togar" (Woronov) who claims The Ramones' music "makes mice explode." The film that asks the musical question, "Is there life after high school?" If the pat and pastoral endings of Fifties and Sixties sock-hop musicals struck an unresolved anarchic chord in many of their viewers, then *High School*'s fadeout of students burning to the ground their prison-of-a-learning-institution should warm their cockles. Every cliché and conceit from those wholesome, old teen rock musicals (and before them, the MGM Mickey-Judy musicals) is used as a springboard for some genuinely inspired satire. As western civilization goes up in flames, so to speak, Joey and The Ramones sing the title tune plus others, including: "Blitzkrieg Bop," "I Just Wanna Have Something To Do," "I Wanna Be Sedated," "I Wanna Be Your Boyfriend," and "Pinhead." Also *heard* over and under the action are such vintage favorites as: "Do You Wanna Dance" (Bobby Freeman); "Did We Meet Somewhere Before?" (Wings); "School Days" (Chuck Berry); "Come Back Jonee" (Devo); and "Rock and Roll" (The Velvet Underground).

***ROD STEWART AND FACES AND KEITH RICHARDS (1977)*** [Rod Stewart, The Faces, Keith Richards]

Concert film of a 1974 Stewart appearance at the Kilburn State Theatre in London. The singer is backed by The Faces—Ron Wood, Ian McLagan, Kenny Jones and Tetsu Yamauchi, and also by Rolling Stone Keith Richards appearing here in a sideman capacity. Songs include: "Maggie May," "Twistin' the Night Away," "Bring It On Home to Me," and "You Send Me."

***ROSE, THE (1979)*** [Bette Midler, Frederic Forrest, Alan Bates]

Overly familiar too-much-too-soon fable of galvanic Sixties rock singer (Midler) and her rise and fall. Unresistant to the worst tendencies of music biopics, the crafters of this *film à clef* of Janis Joplin manage to step into just about every dramatic license trap imaginable. The music's all wrong for the period, and the central character (as written) possesses about as much personal warmth as an iron foundry. One of the few saving graces herein is Bette's interesting, if somewhat overripe, performance in her dramatic debut. Songs include: Amanda McBroom's title tune (a big hit for Bette), "Sold My Soul to Rock and Roll," "Fire Down Below," "Midnight in Memphis," and "When a Man Loves a Woman." Musical arranger and supervisor: Paul Rothchild.

***RUDE BOY (1980)*** [The Clash, Ray Gange]

Mixture of drama, concert movie and cinema verite in biographical study of real life Clash fan, Gange, the rude boy in question. Events depicted in the film go a long way toward demonstrating why our British cousins chatter so much about the "class system." Even the most virulent of The Clash's anti-establishment rhetoric can seem ineffectual at combatting the economic system which perpetually represses the likes of Gange. Well-staged concert sections—and not just arbitrarily slotted into the storyline—feature memorable performances of "London's Burning," "White Riot," "The Prisoner," "Tommy Gun," "All the Young Punks," "Complete Control" and many others.

### SATURDAY NIGHT FEVER (1977) [John Travolta, Barry Miller]

By day a Brooklyn hardware store worker (Travolta) toils away, but come Saturday night, he's king at the local disco. Still, an ambitious young secretary (Karen Lynn Gorney) makes him aware of an even better life that could be awaiting him on the shores of Manhattan. A mere magazine article in *New York Magazine* was the seed kernel of this movie-turned-empire way of life. One of the most successful motion pictures to ever call on the services of rock music for added box office assist, *Fever* almost singlehandedly established John Travolta as a star, re-invented disco, and resurrected the badly sagging career of The Bee Gees—not to mention making a fortune for producer Robert Stigwood that surely (one hopes) exceeded the wildest boundaries of even his imagination. The soundtrack by (among others) Yvonne Elliman, Trammps ("Disco Inferno"), Kool and the Gang ("Open Sesame") and K.C. and the Sunshine Band ("Boogie Shoes"). Bee Gees' titles include: "How Deep Is Your Love?," "Night Fever," "More Than a Woman," and "Staying' Alive"—all massive singles sellers. Additional score by David Shire.

### SECRET POLICEMAN'S OTHER BALL, THE (1979) [Pete Townshend, Tom Robinson, Neil Innes, John Cleese, Clive James, Eleanor Bron, Michael Palin, Terry Jones]

Film of 1979 Amnesty International Comedy Gala at London's Her Majesty's Theatre, with most of the funny business handled by members of the Monty Python comedy group. Musical interludes include a stunning acoustic version of "Won't Get Fooled Again" by Pete Townshend accompanied by classical guitarist, John Williams. Pete also performs "Pinball Wizard" and "Drowned" and Tom Robinson sings "Glad To Be Gay" and "1967 (So Long Ago)."

### SGT. PEPPER'S LONELY HEARTS CLUB BAND (1978) [The Bee Gees, Aerosmith, Alice Cooper, Earth, Wind and Fire, Billy Preston, Stargaard, Peter Frampton, George Burns, Steve Martin]

Film (very) loosely based on songs in the classic Beatles album, with a nod in the direction of *Yellow Submarine*. The Lonely Hearts Club Band, led by "Billy Shears" (Frampton), is infiltrated by villainous agents, "Mean Mr. Mustard" (Frankie Howard) and company, who fall in love with "Strawberry Fields" (Sandy Farina) who. ... For musical authenticity and quasi-officiality, the film's makers called upon the service of Beatles producer emeritus, George Martin. So, on paper, it seemed as if there were simply no way this Robert Stigwood production could fail. But, lo and behold, when it opened in theatres, the film played to half-full houses. The two-record set soundtrack album did just as poorly, although Earth, Wind & Fire had a modest hit with their version of "Got To Get You into My Life." Many notables appear in the grand finale, where "All You Need Is Love" is sung—Donovan, Helen Reddy, Monte Rock III, Dr. John, Wilson Pickett, Minnie Ripperton, Elvin Bishop, Tina Turner, and Frankie Valli among them. Other numbers in this *Pepper* oratorio include "Getting Better" (performed by Peter Frampton and The Bee Gees), "Fixing a Hole" (George Burns), "The Long and Winding Road" (Barry Gibb), "Get Back" (Billy Preston), "Maxwell's Silver Hammer" (Martin) and 22 others.

***SHAKE, RATTLE AND ROCK (1956)*** [Touch Connors, Lisa Gaye, Paul Dubov, Margaret Dumont, Sterling Holloway, Fats Domino, Joe Turner, Tommy Charles, Choker Campbell]

A citizen's group wants to bar rock-and-roll from their Anytown, USA, but a courageous and persistent DJ (Connors) gets some dirt on one of the do-gooders and the day is saved for rock. The finale, where the kids' music is on trial in a televised courtroom scene, is a real howler. The ever-so-avuncular Fats Domino sings "Honey Chile," "I'm in Love Again" and "Ain't that a Shame," and Joe Turner belts out "Feelin' Happy" and "Lipstick, Powder and Paint" in this silly but likeable quickie. One of the very first of the juve-rockers.

***SPEEDWAY (1968)*** [Elvis Presley, Nancy Sinatra]

Heading round the final turn toward the finish line of his film career, Elvis plays what seems like his umpteenth part as a race car driver. This time out, he's a stock car papa who falls in love with an I.R.S. agent (Sinatra) who's hot on his tail over back taxes. Like most of the later Elvis movies, this one comes with all the requisite trimmings of speed, sex, silliness and song, including a duet with Sinatra on "Your Groovy Self." Solo, Elvis sings "There Ain't Nothin Like a Song." Not to be confused with *Spinout*.

***SPINOUT (1966)*** [Elvis Presley, Shelley Fabares]

Silly musical about a singing race car driver (Elvis) and his various romantic involvements. Not to be confused with *Speedway*. Songs include: "Stop, Look and Listen," "Adam and Evil" and the title tune.

***STAR IS BORN, A (1976)*** [Barbra Streisand, Kris Kristofferson, Paul Mazursky, Gary Busey]

A rock superstar on his way down (Kris) helps a young singer on her way up (Barbra), but her love can't save him from self-destruction. This is the second remake of the classic Hollywood tale (not counting the early incarnation entitled *What Price Hollywood*?) and easily the most florid. Moving the action from the movies to the recording industry serves to make it not only louder but bigger. People travel by helicopter, ambulance and mile-long limos over vistas so vast and imposing even de Mille would find them a bit much. As a rocking and rolling "Norman Maine"—here called "John Howard Norman"—Kristofferson seems as much confused by the scale of his surroundings as anything in the plot. Streisand, on the other hand, appears quite at home. Music penned for the film includes material by Kenny Asher and Paul Williams ("Woman on the Moon," "With One More Look at You"), Rupert Holmes ("Queen Bee"), Leon Russell and Barbra Streisand ("Lost Inside of You") and Kenny Loggins and Marilyn and Alan Bergman ("I Believe in Love"). Williams and Streisand co-authored "Evergreen," which won the 1976 Oscar for Best Song.

***STARDUST (1974)*** [David Essex, Adam Faith, Larry Hagman, Keith Moon, Dave Edmunds, Paul Nicholas, Edd Byrnes]

Jim Maclaine (Essex) and his group (The Stray Cats) become an international pop music sensation. Jim, however, is the real drawing card and he soon splits to become an even more successful solo act. Success brings isolation and paranoia fed by drugs, eventually leading the young star to an early grave. Sixteen minutes were lopped off for the American release of this rise-of-a-rock-star musical drama from Britain, thus somewhat diminishing its overall effectiveness. What remains—even in the truncated version—is still extremely affecting. Very close to being a bio of The Beatles (although elements of the careers of other superstars are interleaved) it captures much of the atmosphere of splenderous seclusion of the higher echelons of the rock world. Faith's portrayal of Essex's sexually ambiguous manager is a standout in this sequel to the far more modestly scaled *That'll Be the Day*. Music and songs by Dave Edmunds and David Puttnam.

## STAYING ALIVE (1983)

Near disastrous attempt at a sequel to *Saturday Night Fever*, John Travolta returns as a would-be professional dancer in Manhattan. His raw sexual energy (with newly muscled, sleek body developed under the direction of Sylvester Stallone, who co-wrote, co-produced and directed) was best part of film. The two love interests were the sweet, loving chorus girl, played by Cynthia Rhodes, and the bitchy star, played by Finola Hughes. The grand finale featured an elaborate production number called "Satan's Alley"—an unsuccessful blending of Broadway and rock styles. Songs by The Bee Gees, "The Woman in You," "Stayin' Alive" and by Sylvester's brother, Frank, "Far from Over."

## STREETS OF FIRE (1984)

Called a "rock fable," this film was an attempt to mix western film clichés with rock music. Michael Paré plays hero aptly named "Cody." Heroine (Diane Lane) is rock singer kidnapped by motorcycle gang. No relation to Springsteen song of same title. With lots of sexual and physical violence and a score by Ry Cooder, film failed to find an audience.

## TAMI SHOW, THE (1965) [The Beach Boys, Chuck Berry, James Brown and the Famous Flames, The Barbarians, Marvin Gaye, Gerry and the Pacemakers, Lesley Gore, Jan and Dean, Billy J. Kramer and the Dakotas, Smokey Robinson and the Miracles, The Supremes, The Rolling Stones, The Blossoms]

One for the time capsules! The greatest gathering of rock performers ever assembled for one film, *Woodstock* and *Monterey Pop* notwithstanding. All in performance at the Santa Monica (California) Civic auditorium, October 24, 1964. While the original videotape stock of this film (which is discussed more fully in the main text of this book) lacks a *Woodstock*'s visual resources, *TAMI* makes up for these failings with its own wit, verve and talent. Musical highlights include: The Supremes' "Where Did Our Love Go?" and "Baby Love"; The Stones' "Around and Around" and "Off the Hook"; Brown's "Please Please Me"; Berry's "Johnny B. Goode"; Gaye's "Can I Get a Witness" and Smokey's "Mickey's Monkey." Note: currently circulating versions of *TAMI* lack the Beach Boys sequence, which has been deleted due to contractual reasons.

## THIS IS SPINAL TAP (1984)

A parody of heavy metal band's decline from superstardom written and performed by Christopher Guest, Michael McKean, Harry Shearer and Rob Reiner, who also directed. This mock-documentary follows a British band's tour of America in the declining stages of their career. This hilarious satire of the record industry actually led to a demand for the band on television and in concert. Soundtrack album of the same name written by the stars of the film.

### TO RUSSIA...WITH ELTON (1979) [Elton John]

Elton John sings for the borscht and babushka set in docu of singer's 1979 tour of Soviet Union. Film narrated by Dudley Moore, features E.J., feathers and all, doing "Crocodile Rock," "Rocketman," and, fittingly, "Back in the U.S.S.R." and other hits before austere and confused-looking crowds in Moscow and Leningrad.

### TOMMY (1975) [Ann-Margret, Roger Daltrey, Oliver Reed, Jack Nicholson, Tina Turner, Elton John, Eric Clapton, Keith Moon, Pete Townshend, John Entwistle, Arthur Brown]

A blind, deaf and dumb pinball champion becomes the leader of a religious cult. Initially growing out of a Who jam session, the first stage was the recording – the first (so-called) "rock opera." Then it went through several theatrical metamorphoses (a ballet and quasi-musical) and became an even bigger phenomenon. Then it touched down on the stage of New York City's Metropolitan Opera in a performance by The Who themselves. A film, then, was inevitable; and who but Ken Russell could have created the form that finally transformed the project into the maddest, most eccentric movie musical since *Yolanda and the Thief*. Somehow, this all-star rock gala just manages to work – even down to the shot of Ann-Margaret (who plays Tommy's mother) rolling around in a veritable lava flow of baked beans pouring out of a busted television set. Elton John's rendition of "Pinball Wizard" (in giant platform shoes) is a musical high point, and Tina Turner simply *is* "The Acid Queen" in the most genuinely terrifying production number ever made. Other hits include "See Me Feel Me," "I'm Free," "We're Not Gonna Take It" and "Eyesight to the Blind" (which unlike the other Who-penned numbers was written by Sonny Boy Williamson). Ann-Margaret's number, "The Day It Rained Champagne," was especially written by The Who for this film.

### TWIST AROUND THE CLOCK (1961) [Chubby Checker, Vicki Spencer, Dion, The Marcels]

The birth of the twist as told through the eyes of Hollywood, as twist prophet Checker comes down from the mount to spread the gospel of the latest dance craze to urban swingers. With this film, producer Katzman proved, five years after his phenomenal success with *Rock Around the Clock*, that he still had the magic touch and could ride the crest of a craze with the best of 'em. This formula quickie

*Mick Jagger*

cleaned up at the box office quite nicely. Chubby sings "Twistin' U.S.A.," "Don't Twist with Anybody Else But Me," the title tune and several others. Dion does "The Wanderer" and The Marcels reprise their "Blue Moon."

**200 MOTELS (1971)** [Frank Zappa and the Mothers of Invention, Mark Volman, Keith Moon, Ringo Starr]

Surrealistic fable of musician's life "on the road" details frantic goings-on as Zappa and the Mothers touch down in "Centerville, U.S.A." Zappa employed all the state-of-the-art video equipment he could lay his hands on for this cartoony tale. Computer graphics, animation (the self-enclosed seg "Dental Hygiene Dilemma" is a knockout) and the purposely flat stage sets combine to make this film totally infectious and engaging. The nearly nonstop score, much of it played by the Royal Philharmonic Orchestra and Chorus, was all written by Zappa. Big things were expected for *200 Motels* when it was released, but it came and went very quickly.

**UNION CITY (1980)** [Debbie Harry, Pat Benatar, Dennis Lipscomb]

Debbie Harry plays the wife of a milquetoast who impulsively kills a man, and then proceeds to keep the body hidden in an adjacent apartment. Failed Fassbinder-ish version of a Cornell Wollrich story, features a decent dramatic debut by the lead singer of Blondie. That group's Chris Stein also did the music. Pat Benatar appears in a brief role.

**VELVET UNDERGROUND AND NICO, THE (1966)** [The Velvet Underground, Nico]

Film of The Velvet Underground at Sixties scenemaker spa, The Dom, also features appearances by actress Mary Woronov and poet Gerard Malanga.

**VIVA LAS VEGAS! (1964)** [Elvis Presley, Ann-Margret]

"It's That Go-Go Guy and That Bye Bye (Birdie) Gal in the Fun Capital of the World!" Elvis in yet another role as a race car driver who, this time out, succumbs to the tight curves of Ann-Margret. This is Presley's last good musical, thanks to the contributions of the sensational A-M and director Sidney. Even here the boy from Tupelo looks a trifle tired, but when Ann-Margret flings down the dancing gauntlet in their duet on "C'mon Everybody," Elvis (as of yore) rises to the occasion. Other songs include: "If You Think I Need You," "What'd I Say" and the title tune.

**WHERE THE BOYS ARE (1960)** [Connie Francis, Yvette Mimieux, Paula Prentiss, Dolores Hart]

Four young women (*near*-teenagers) visit the Ft. Lauderdale Easter vacation revels and test reality during their first time away from school and family. No rock-and-roll here, unless one charitably counts Francis as a rocker, but this MGM first-of-its-kind big budget musical proved that there was an endless supply of gold to be mined from the youth movie market. The lesson learned was that the more money you put in, the more you take out at the box office, for this film was a huge hit. Soon, everybody re-thought their approach to kids and movies and rock films began to take on a whole new, more expensive look. Connie sings the title tune.

*Elvis Presley, "Wild In The Country"*

**WILD IN THE COUNTRY (1961)** [Elvis Presley, Tuesday Weld, Hope Lange, Millie Perkins]

Rebel without a pause. Presley is involved with *three* love interests in this story of a "misunderstood" youth who gets back on the right track with the help of one of his amours, psychologist Lange. Weld plays gal friend number two, a high school hellcat, and Perkins is the girl-next-door. The film started out as a well-intentioned one, with a Clifford Odets class-act script, but by the time Fox moguls got finished tampering with it, all the toughness was beaten out. Songs were added ("I Slipped, Stumbled and Fell," "Lonely Man," "In My Way" and the title tune), and the film ended up trying to function both as a high fallutin' drama and as a standard Presley musical. One of the most confused and confusing of all of the singer's movie efforts.

**WOODSTOCK (1970)** [Joan Baez, Joe Cocker, Country Joe and the Fish, Crosby, Stills, Nash & Young, Arlo Guthrie, Richie Havens, Jimi Hendrix, Santana, John Sebastian, Sha-Na-Na, Sly and the Family Stone, Ten Years After, The Who]

*And featuring!* a half-million young, mud-covered, blissed-out, free-loving charter members of what would come to be called "the Woodstock nation." Documentary of the 1969 Woodstock Music Festival — actually called a "music and art fair," though hardly anyone remembers it by that name. Almost everybody recalls the facts arising out of the fest, however, i.e., "x" amount of births, deaths, traffic jams, O.D.'s, etc. Easily the most publicized media event since the birth of Little Ricky Ricardo, this celluloid memento, highlighted by split-screen techniques, superimpositions and ear-splitting stereophonic sound could be described as The Triumph of The Will of youth culture. The Who's *Tommy* medley and Hendrix's "Star-Spangled Banner," both preserved here, are great moments in rock on film in an over-three-hours extravaganza that also features Joe Cocker singing "With a Little Help from My Friends," "Higher" by Sly Stone and CSN&Y doing Joni Mitchell's "Woodstock." Note: A shortened and bowdlerized version of this film, entitled *Woodstock Remembered*, began appearing on TV in 1981.

**YELLOW SUBMARINE (1968)**

The Beatles to the rescue as the mythical kingdom of Pepperland is invaded by the Blue Meanies, who want to purge the world of fun and music. The speaking voices of JPG&R dubbed by actors in this elaborate animated feature produced by Apple Films — but the music is pure Beatles. New songs written expressly for the project: "Only a Northern Song," "Altogether Now," "Hey, Bulldog," "It's All Too Much," plus previous Beatle hits like "All You Need Is Love," "Nowhere Man," and "Lucy in the Sky with Diamonds," served up with appropriate images designed by master animator, George Dunning. Additional musical score by George Martin. Note: "Hey Bulldog" dropped from final American release print.

## *25 favorite video clips*

- **BEAT IT**
  Michael Jackson

- **BILLIE JEAN**
  Michael Jackson

- **PRESSURE**
  Billy Joel

- **ROCKIT**
  Herbie Hancock

- **EVERY BREATH YOU TAKE**
  The Police

- **COME DANCING**
  The Kinks

- **SHE WORKS HARD FOR THE MONEY**
  Donna Summer

- **CHINA GIRL**
  David Bowie

- **I LOVE L.A.**
  Randy Newman

- **SHOCK THE MONKEY**
  Peter Gabriel

- **HUNGRY LIKE THE WOLF**
  Duran Duran

- **GIRLS JUST WANNA HAVE FUN**
  Cyndi Lauper

- **SHE BLINDED ME WITH SCIENCE**
  Thomas Dolby

- **TV DINNERS**
  ZZ Top

Donna Summer

- **THRILLER**
  Michael Jackson

- **SWEET DREAMS**
  Eurythmics

- **EAT IT**
  Weird Al Yankovic

- **BURNING DOWN THE HOUSE**
  Talking Heads

- **DANCING WITH MYSELF**
  Billy Idol

*Cyndi Lauper*

*The Police*

- **BEAST OF BURDEN**
  Bette Midler

- **WHO CAN IT BE NOW?**
  Men at Work

- **LET'S DANCE**
  David Bowie

- **MISS ME BLIND**
  Culture Club

- **SYNCHRONICITY**
  The Police

- **FOR THE LONGEST TIME**
  Billy Joel

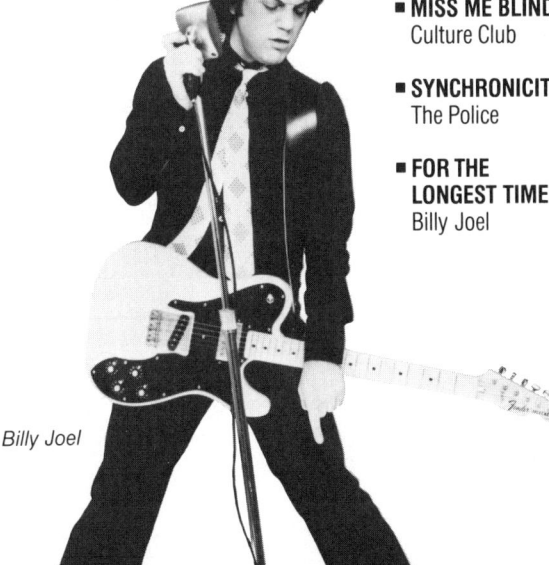

*Billy Joel*

# ROCK BIRTHDAYS

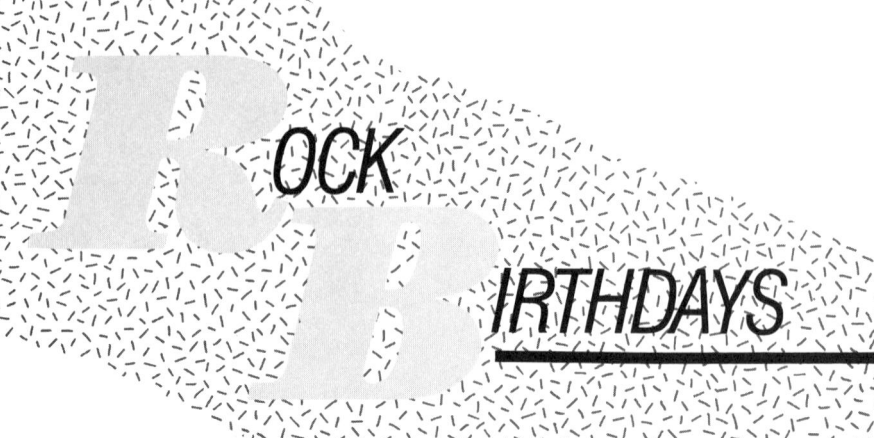

**JANUARY 3, 1926**

**George Martin:** London, England. Best known as record producer for **The Beatles**. Also noted for successful productions for **Jeff Beck**, **America**, and **The Little River Band**.

**JANUARY 3, 1945**

**Steve Stills:** Dallas, Texas. Founder of **Buffalo Springfield**, then partner in supergroup **Crosby, Stills, Nash & Young** before engaging in various solo projects.

**JANUARY 3, 1946**

**John Paul Jones**, born John Baldwin: Kent, England. Producer / arranger / bassist / keyboardist for **Led Zeppelin**. Recording session credits include work with **The Rolling Stones, Donovan, Dusty Springfield**, and **Herman's Hermits**.

**JANUARY 7, 1944**

**Mike McCartney:** Liverpool, England. The brother of **Beatle Paul** formed a satirical group, **Scaffold**, using the name Mike McGear and had a Number 1 hit in England in 1968, "Lily the Pink."

**JANUARY 7, 1948**

**Kenny Loggins:** Everett, Washington. Moderately successful as a songwriter for **The Nitty Gritty Dirt Band** and in 1970, half of **Loggins & Messina**. After the breakup with **Jim Messina** in 1976, even more successful as a solo artist.

**JANUARY 8, 1935**

**Elvis Aron Presley:** Tupelo, Mississippi. Singer, guitarist, songwriter, and film star. From his "Heartbreak Hotel" in 1955 to more record sales than any other recording artist (over 500 million) and more than 30 film appearances. Credited as "The King" of rock 'n' roll.

### JANUARY 8, 1947

**David Bowie**, born David Robert Jones: London, England. To avoid confusion with **Davey Jones** of **The Monkees**, he changed his name to Bowie in 1968 and has since recorded several successful LPs including *Ziggy Stardust*, *Young Americans* and *Scary Monsters*. His stage credits include *The Elephant Man* on Broadway and in film, *The Man Who Fell to Earth*.

### JANUARY 9, 1941

**Joan Baez:** Staten Island, New York. Singer-guitarist known as "Queen of Protest" for her anti-war and civil rights work in the Sixties and early Seventies.

### JANUARY 9, 1945

**James Patrick Page:** Middlesex, England. Originally a London session player, Page joined **The Yardbirds** as a replacement for **Jeff Beck** and in 1968 formed **Led Zeppelin**. His independent recording projects include the movie soundtrack for *Death Wish II*.

### JANUARY 9, 1950

**David Johansen.** Former guitarist-vocalist with **The New York Dolls**, later embarking on a successful solo career.

### JANUARY 10, 1943

**Jim Croce:** Philadelphia, Pennsylvania. Singer and songwriter who grabbed national attention in 1972 with "Don't Mess Around with Jim" and "Bad Bad Leroy Brown" after nearly a decade of musical obscurity. Croce died in a plane crash in Louisiana in 1973.

### JANUARY 10, 1945

**Rod Stewart:** Glasgow, Scotland. Discovered while playing harmonica on a train platform by legendary bluesman **Long John Baldry**. Began singing career with **Hoochie Coochie Men** before joining **Jeff Beck Group**, then **Small Faces**. His solo career started in 1969 and has moved through a string of Gold and Platinum albums.

### JANUARY 10, 1952

**Pat Benatar:** Long Island, New York. Operatic student turned rock singer, discovered while waitressing at the New York comedy club Catch a Rising Star, where she auditioned on amateur nights. Her debut LP bore the hit single "Heartbreaker" and she's been awarded two consecutive Grammys.

### JANUARY 10, 19?

**Donald Fagen.** Founding member of **Steely Dan**, a studio-oriented rock-jazz influenced group with Platinum credentials.

### JANUARY 15, 1949

**Ronnie Van Zandt:** Jacksonville, Florida. Founding member of **Lynyrd Skynyrd**. Singer-songwriter on such hits as "Sweet Home Alabama" and "Free Bird" before his death in a plane crash in 1977.

*JANUARY 17, 1948*

**Mick Taylor:** Hertfordshire, England. Originally a member of **John Mayall**'s **Bluesbreakers**, Taylor replaced **Brian Jones** as guitarist for **The Rolling Stones** in 1969. Known as the only member of The Stones to "leave the band alive," Taylor joined the **Jack Bruce Band** in 1974 for a short-lived stint and now records solo and makes occasional guest appearances on LPs by other artists.

*JANUARY 19, 1939*

**Phil Everly:** Brownie, Kentucky. With brother **Don**, **The Everly Brothers** were formed in 1957. The first hit single, "Bye Bye Love," sparks a career which lasts on and off until 1973. In September, 1983, The Everly Brothers reunite for two historic concerts at London's Royal Albert Hall which leads to *The Everly Brothers Reunion Concert* TV special and *The Everly Brothers Rock 'n' Roll Odyssey* TV documentary, followed by a nationwide 1984 summer concert tour and release of a new album.

*JANUARY 19, 1943*

**Janis Joplin:** Port Arthur, Texas. Began singing on the local bar circuit at 17 before joining **Big Brother and the Holding Company** in 1966. Attracted worldwide attention with an appearance at the Monterey Pop Festival, followed by a solo career in 1968 and death in 1970.

*JANUARY 19, 1949*

**Robert Palmer:** Yorkshire, England. Singer and guitarist first with **Vinegar Joe**, then as solo artist in 1973 leaning heavily on R&B-flavored rock.

*JANUARY 20, 1952*

**Paul Stanley:** New York City. Co-founder of the theatrical rock group **Kiss**. Kiss members, pre-1984, never appeared without makeup but now show their faces.

*JANUARY 21, 1941*

**Richie Havens:** New York City. Fast-strumming folk singer who made his mark in the late Sixties with anti-war songs and particularly with his appearance at Woodstock.

*JANUARY 22, 1935*

**Sam Cooke:** Chicago, Illinois. One of the most popular R&B pop singers of the Fifties and Sixties, Cooke started singing gospel and later recorded his own songs, including "Shake" and "You Send Me." He died of gunshot wounds in Los Angeles in 1964.

*Don and Phil Everly*

**JANUARY 22, 1953**
**Steve Perry.** Lead singer of **Journey.** Released a solo LP in 1984 entitled *Street Talk.*

**JANUARY 24, 1947**
**Warren Zevon.** Satirical rock singer, songwriter and keyboard player. Late seventies FM hits include "Werewolves of London" and "Excitable Boy."

**JANUARY 24, 1949**
**John Belushi**: Chicago, Illinois. A comic actor made famous by TV's *Saturday Night Live*, he and **Dan Aykroyd** formed **The Blues Brothers** in the late Seventies and scored a hit with "Soul Man." Belushi died in 1982.

**JANUARY 25, 19?**
**Anita Pallenberg.** Girlfriend of **Rolling Stone Brian Jones**, then **Keith Richards**, by whom she bore son **Marlon**. Co-starred with **Mick Jagger** in the film *Performance*.

**JANUARY 25, 19?**
**China.** Daughter of **Grace Slick** and **Paul Kantner** of **The Jefferson Airplane/Starship.** Was to be named God but parents opted for China, a name that could be changed again "to something more normal as she gets older, if she wants to."

**JANUARY 28, 1982**
**Ryan Daniel Browne.** First child of **Jackson Browne** and wife, **Lynne Sweeney**.

**JANUARY 29, 1952**
**Tommy Ramone**: New York City. Drummer for **The Ramones**, formed in 1974. The band got its start playing the same New York club circuit from which emerged **Patti Smith** and **Talking Heads**.

**JANUARY 31, 1951**
**Phil Collins**: London, England. Drummer and vocalist for **Genesis**, replacing **John Mayhew** in 1970. Moved to lead vocals with the departure of **Peter Gabriel** and has since developed successful solo LPs and brought Genesis to the top of the charts.

**JANUARY 31, 1956**
**Johnny "Rotten" Lydon**: London, England. Notorious leader of **The Sex Pistols** and then **Public Image Limited**.

**FEBRUARY 1, 1937**
**Don Everly**: Brownie, Kentucky. He and brother **Phil** formed **The Everly Brothers**.

### FEBRUARY 1, 1968
**Lisa Marie Presley**: Memphis, Tennessee. Born to **Elvis** and **Priscilla** at Baptist Memorial Hospital. As heir to her father's estate, Lisa can collect on her 24th birthday, 1992.

### FEBRUARY 2, 1942
**Graham Nash**: Lancashire, England. Singer and guitarist with **The Hollies** before becoming part of **Crosby, Stills & Nash** in 1969. Various solo albums.

### FEBRUARY 3, 1947
**Dave Davies**: London, England. With brother **Ray** founds **The Kinks** in 1964 and he continues as guitarist.

### FEBRUARY 4, 1948
**Alice Cooper**, born Vincent Furnier: Detroit, Michigan. He's best known for his theatrical rock antics with snakes and the hits "Eighteen," "School's Out," and "Welcome to My Nightmare."

### FEBRUARY 5, 1945
**Bob Marley**: Middlesex, Jamaica. Singer and guitarist credited with bringing reggae to the world's rock fans. Formed **The Wailers** in 1965 and remained with them until his death in 1981.

### FEBRUARY 6, 1943
**Fabian**, born Fabiano Forte: Philadelphia, Pennsylvania. A teenage heart-throb of the Fifties, he had a big hit in 1959 with "I'm a Man."

### FEBRUARY 9, 1941
**Carole King**, born Carole Klein: Brooklyn, New York. Singer and songwriter who penned hits for various artists in the late Fifties and Sixties, until her solo career in 1971. Best known for her hugely successful LP *Tapestry*.

### FEBRUARY 10, 1940
**Roberta Flack**: Asheville, North Carolina. Singer and pianist with a strong solo career and duet history with **Donny Hathaway**. Best known for "Killing Me Softly with His Song," soundtrack theme for **Clint Eastwood**'s *Play Misty for Me*.

### FEBRUARY 11, 1935
**Gene Vincent**, born Vincent Eugene Craddock: Norfolk, Virginia. Noted contemporary of **Elvis Presley** and one of the first "grease and leather" rockers.

### FEBRUARY 12, 1935
**Ray Manzarek**: Chicago, Illinois. Keyboard player for **The Doors**.

### FEBRUARY 15, 1951
**Melissa Manchester**: Bronx, New York. Singer and songwriter with an early background in **The Harlettes**, then success as a solo performer.

### FEBRUARY 16, 1935

**Sonny Bono**, born Salvatore Bono: Detroit, Michigan. Singer and songwriter in partnership with wife **Cher** for "I Got You Babe" in 1964, and later with "The Beat Goes On." **Sonny and Cher** hosted a weekly TV show in the early Seventies before splitting up both personally and professionally in 1974 to pursue solo careers.

### FEBRUARY 18, 1933

**Yoko Ono Lennon**: Tokyo, Japan. Meets **John Lennon** and is married in 1969. Various recordings with Lennon after **Beatles** breakup in 1970.

### FEBRUARY 20, 1946

**J. Geils**. Guitarist who weathered the Boston club scene for years with the **J. Geils Band** before reaching stardom with the *Freeze Frame* LP in 1982.

### FEBRUARY 21, 1943

**David Geffen**. Formed Geffen Records in the early Eighties and signs **John Lennon** and **Elton John** as its first artists.

### FEBRUARY 23, 1944

**Johnny Winter**: Leland, Mississippi. Guitarist with Delta blues background who has collaborated often with brother **Edgar Winter**.

### FEBRUARY 24, 1944

**Paul Jones:** Portsmouth, England. Original singer for **Manfred Mann**'s **Earth Band** through the early Seventies.

### FEBRUARY 25, 1943

**George Harrison:** Liverpool, England. Guitarist with **The Beatles**, he met **John Lennon** and **Paul McCartney** in 1960. Continued success as a solo artist following The Beatles' breakup ten years later.

### FEBRUARY 26, 1928

**Antoine "Fats" Domino**: New Orleans, Louisiana. Legendary singer and piano player who influenced many rock styles of the Fifties and Sixties with his upbeat keyboard work. Best known for his hits, "Blueberry Hill," "Josephine," "Walking to New Orleans."

### FEBRUARY 26, 1932

**Johnny Cash**: Dyess, Arkansas. Singer and guitarist with early recordings on the Sun label, including "I Walk the Line," later a major country star of TV and films.

### FEBRUARY 27, 1959

**Steve Allen Lewis**. Son of **Jerry Lee Lewis**, named for TV comedian-host **Steve Allen**. Allen gave Jerry Lee one of the early breaks in his career.

*James Taylor*

**FEBRUARY 28, 1942**

**Brian Jones**: Cheltenham Spa, England. Guitarist for **The Rolling Stones** until he exited the band in June, 1969. He drowned a month later.

**MARCH 1, 1944**

**Roger Daltrey**: London, England. Lead singer and founding member of **The Who** with **Pete Townshend**, **Keith Moon** and **John Entwhistle**. His solo career includes film roles in *Tommy* and *McVicar*.

**MARCH 2, 1943**

**George Benson**: Pittsburgh, Pennsylvania. Jazz guitarist and vocalist with successes in the Seventies for "This Masquerade" and "On Broadway."

**MARCH 2, 1944**

**Lou Reed**: New York City. Singer and guitarist with **John Cale**, then formed **The Velvet Underground** in the mid-Sixties and later pursued a solo career. Best known for "Walk on the Wild Side" and "Sweet Jane."

**MARCH 2, 1949**

**Rory Gallagher**: Ballyshannon, Ireland. Blues guitarist for **Taste** in 1968, with prominent solo career following.

**MARCH 4, 1944**

**Mary Wilson**: Detroit, Michigan. Founding member of **The Supremes** with **Diana Ross** and **Flo Ballard**.

**MARCH 4, 1948**

**Chris Squire**: London, England. Bassist for **Yes** and co-founder of the group until their breakup in 1968. Formed **Asia** in 1982, the short-lived group, then reformed Yes in 1983.

**MARCH 6, 1947**

**David Gilmour**: Cambridge, England. Guitarist for **Pink Floyd** at the invitation of founder **Syd Barrett**. Pink Floyd disbands after the huge success of their double album, *The Wall* and Gilmour embarks on a solo career in 1983.

**MARCH 7, 1946**

**Peter Wolf**. Singer for **The J. Geils Band** after an early career with the **Hallucinations**, Wolf exits the J. Geils Band in 1983 to begin a solo career.

**MARCH 9, 1945**

**Robin Trower**: London, England. Original member of **Procol Harum**, then **Jude**, and evolving into a solo career as a guitarist. Best known for LP *Bridge of Sighs*.

### MARCH 12, 1948

**James Taylor**: Boston, Massachusetts. Singer and songwriter who joined with **Danny Kortchmar** to form **The Flying Machine** in 1966. His solo successes have been numerous since *Sweet Baby James* in 1968.

### MARCH 13, 1939

**Neil Sedaka**: New York City. Singer and concert pianist as a child, a songwriter for other artists until recording "Oh! Carol!" in 1959 and enjoying a successful solo career.

### MARCH 15, 1941

**Mike Love**: Los Angeles, California. With cousins **Brian**, **Carl**, and **Dennis Wilson**, he forms **Carl & the Passions**, then **Kenny and the Cadets** before making history as **The Beach Boys**' lead singer.

### MARCH 15, 1944

**Sly Stone**, born Sylvester Stewart: Dallas, Texas. Formed **Sly and the Family Stone** after beginning with the Viscanes. Career highlights include Woodstock.

### MARCH 15, 1947

**Ry Cooder**: Los Angeles, California. Guitarist with **Rising Sun** and **Taj Mahal**, then with **Captain Beefheart's Magic Band**. Currently pursues a solo career and occasional session work.

### MARCH 16, 1942

**Jerry Jeff Walker**: New York City. Singer and guitarist noted for work with **Circus Maximus** and the rendition of his own "Mr. Bojangles."

### MARCH 16, 1954

**Nancy Wilson**: Vancouver, B.C., Canada. With sister **Ann** develops **Heart** into major act in the Seventies, winning hit status the first time on record with "Magic Man."

### MARCH 17, 1942

**Paul Kantner**: San Francisco, California. Singer, guitarist and founding member of **Jefferson Airplane**, then **Jefferson Starship**. A variety of other music projects including *Blows Against the Empire*.

### MARCH 20, 1950

**Carl Palmer**: Bournemouth, England. Drummer with **The Crazy World of Arthur Brown** until he formed **Atomic Rooster** and **Emerson, Lake & Palmer**. In 1982, new success with the supergroup **Asia**.

*George Benson*

### MARCH 22, 1948
**Andrew Lloyd Webber**: London, England. Composer of *Jesus Christ Superstar* and *Evita*.

### MARCH 29, 1947
**Bobby Kimbal**. Lead singer with **Toto** and hits "Hold the Line" and "Rosanna."

### MARCH 30, 1945
**Eric Clapton:** Surrey, England. Guitarist with an early career in **John Mayall**'s **Bluesbreakers**, **The Yardbirds**, **Cream**, **Blind Faith** and **Derek & the Dominos** before settling down to solo work.

### APRIL 1, 1948
**Ronnie Lane:** London, England. Bassist for **Small Faces**, then **The Faces** with **Rod Stewart** before soloing with **Ronnie Lane's Slim Chance**.

### APRIL 2, 1939
**Marvin Gaye:** Washington, D.C. Singer and instrumentalist son of a minister, known for his Sixties hit singles and LPs, including "I Heard It Through the Grapevine." On April 1, 1984 Gaye is shot and killed by his father in a family dispute. His death shocks the nation.

### APRIL 2, 1941
**Leon Russell**: Lawton, Oklahoma. Singer and keyboard player for **Jerry Lee Lewis**, **Joe Cocker**, **The Byrds**, **The Rolling Stones** and **George Harrison** before forming his own Shelter Records in 1969.

### APRIL 2, 1948
**Emmylou Harris**: Birmingham, Alabama. Singer and guitarist popular for her association with **Gram Parsons**, **Linda Ronstadt**, **Little Feat**, **John Sebastian** and **Bob Dylan**, as well as numerous solo works.

### APRIL 4, 1915
**Muddy Waters**, born McKinley Morganfield: Rolling Fork, Mississippi. Blues singer and guitarist who began a recording career in 1941 and was a major influence on many of today's rock musicians. Waters dies on April 30, 1983 of a cardiac arrest in his home in Illinois.

### APRIL 5, 1946
**Jane Asher**, sister of singer-producer **Peter Asher** and one-time fiancee of **Paul McCartney**.

### APRIL 5, 1950
**Agnetha "Anna" Ulvaeus**: Stockholm, Sweden. Singer with hugely successful **Abba**.

*APRIL 6, 19?*

**Michelle Phillips**, born Michelle Gilliam: Long Beach, California. Singer with **The Mamas and the Papas** and one-time wife of Papa **John Phillips**.

*APRIL 7, 1915*

**Billie Holiday**: Baltimore, Maryland. Blues singer considered to be the greatest female vocalist of the genre, characterized in film by **Diana Ross** in *Lady Sings the Blues*.

*APRIL 7, 1920*

**Ravi Shankar**: India. Sitarist and mentor to **George Harrison**.

*APRIL 7, 1949*

**John Oates**: New York City. Guitarist and singing partner with **Daryl Hall** in **Hall and Oates**.

*APRIL 7, 1951*

**Janis Ian**: New York City. Singer and songwriter who recorded her first hit at age 15 and continues to perform as a solo artist.

*APRIL 8, 1947*

**Steve Howe**: London, England. Guitarist for **Yes** from 1971 until its demise in 1981, then joined supergroup **Asia**.

*APRIL 8, 1963*

**Julian Lennon**: Liverpool, England. Son of **John Lennon** by his first wife **Cynthia**, and drummer on the final track of the *Walls and Bridges* LP.

*APRIL 10, 1932*

**Carl Perkins**: Tipton County, Tennessee. Singer and songwriter of "Blue Suede Shoes" and other hits, both rock and country.

*APRIL 12, 1954*

**Pat Travers**: Toronto, Canada. Singer and featured solo guitarist in the band that bears his name.

*APRIL 13, 1944*

**Jack Casady**: Washington, D. C. Bassist and founding member of **Jefferson Airplane** and then **Hot Tuna**.

*APRIL 15, 1944*

**Dave Edmunds**: Cardiff, Wales. Singer and guitarist with **Love Sculpture** in the mid-Seventies, but best known for his teaming with **Nick Lowe** in **Rockpile** and various solo projects.

*APRIL 21, 1947*

**Iggy Pop**, born James Jewel Osterburg: Ann Arbor, Michigan. Founding member of **The Stooges** in the late Sixties with various appearances on **David Bowie** tours, remembered mostly for his outrageous stage antics.

*APRIL 23, 1936*

**Roy Orbison**: Vernon, Texas. Singer, songwriter and guitarist best known for his hits "Pretty Woman" and "Only the Lonely."

*APRIL 26, 1938*

**Duane Eddy**: Corning, New York. Guitarist and songwriter noted for pop-rock instrumentals "Rebel Rouser" and "Peter Gunn" in the Fifties.

*APRIL 27, 1951*

**Paul "Ace" Frehly**: Bronx, New York. Guitarist with **Kiss**.

*MAY 1, 1939*

**Judy Collins**: Seattle, Washington. Singer and songwriter, instrumental in the discovery of **Joni Mitchell** and **Randy Newman**; the object of affection in "Suite: Judy Blue Eyes" by **Crosby, Stills & Nash**. Best known for the hits "Both Sides Now" and "Someday Soon."

*MAY 3, 1919*

**Pete Seeger**: New York City. Noted as father of the early Sixties folk and environmental movement, with more than fifty LPs recorded during his career.

*MAY 3, 1928*

**James Brown**: Macon, Georgia. Singer and songwriter celebrated as the "King of Rhythm, Blues and Funk" for his dynamic but outrageous stage performances with **The Fabulous Flames**.

*MAY 3, 1937*

**Frankie Valli**, born Frank Castelluccio: Newark, New Jersey. Lead singer and founder of **The Four Seasons**.

*MAY 3, 1945*

**Bob Seger**: Ann Arbor, Michigan. Superstar singer, guitarist and keyboard player who formed **The Bob Seger System** in 1968; had an enormous resurgence in popularity in the late Seventies with **The Silver Bullet Band** and the hit LP *Night Moves*.

*MAY 4, 1951*

**Jackie Jackson**: Gary, Indiana. Singer with **The Jacksons**.

*MAY 7, 19?*

**Derek Taylor**: England. Publicist and record executive responsible for the first press images of **The Beatles**; later a top executive with Warner/Elektra/Asylum Records.

*MAY 8, 1944*

**Gary Glitter**, born Paul Gadd: Oxfordshire, England. Singer best known in the early Seventies for "Rock and Roll, Parts 1 & 2."

*MAY 10, 1945*

**Dave Mason**: Worcester, England. Singer and guitarist with various groups before joining **Traffic** in 1968. His solo career has been punctuated with a number of hits.

*MAY 10, 1957*

**Sid Vicious**: England. Bassist with **The Sex Pistols** as replacement for **Glen Matlock** in 1977. Arrested and tried for the murder of his girlfriend before taking his own life.

*MAY 12, 1948*

**Steve Winwood**: Birmingham, England. Singer, producer, multi-instrumentalist who joined **The Spencer Davis Group** at age 15, writing and singing "I'm a Man" and "Gimme Some Lovin'." He founded **Traffic** in two incarnations with a stopover with **Eric Clapton** in **Blind Faith** in between. Had a short career with the band **GO** in 1976 before emerging with a successful solo career in the Eighties and the hit LP *Arc of a Diver*.

*MAY 12, 1946*

**Ian McLagan**: England. Keyboardist for **Small Faces**, then **Faces** until its demise in 1978. A well known soloist and session player.

*MAY 13, 1950*

**Stevie Wonder**, born Steveland Morris Hardaway: Detroit, Michigan. Singer, songwriter and multi-instrumentalist already well known before his teens for his singing and harmonica talents. Wonder's prolific career has produced scores of Grammy awards and hits including "You Are the Sunshine of My Life" and "Superstition."

*MAY 13, 1950*

**Peter Gabriel**: London, England. Singer, producer, multi-instrumentalist and songwriter, founder of **Genesis** in 1969 as theatrical lead singer. Solo successes after his departure from Genesis in 1975, most notably "Salisbury Hill."

*MAY 14, 1936*

**Bobby Darin**, born Robert Cassotto: New York City. Teen idol of the late Fifties and early Sixties with pop hits "Splish Splash" and particularly "Mack the Knife."

*MAY 14, 1943*

**Jack Bruce**: Glasgow, Scotland. Bassist and singer first with **Alexis Korner** and **John Mayall** before forming **Cream** with **Eric Clapton** in 1966. Bruce formed **Bruce, West and Laing** in between various solo projects.

*MAY 15, 1948*

**Brian Eno**: England. Singer, songwriter and multi-instrumentalist noted for co-founding **Roxy Music**, which he left after the second LP to form his own Obscure Records. Eno has close associations with **David Bowie, Robert Fripp, John Cale** and **Talking Heads**.

*MAY 15, 1974*

**Ahment Rodan**. Son of **Frank Zappa**.

*MAY 17, 1942*

**Taj Mahal**: New York City. Singer, songwriter, producer and multi-instrumentalist who started with **The Rising Sons**, a band that included **Ry Cooder**. Taj recorded numerous LPs for Columbia Records in the Sixties and early Seventies and has film credits that include *Sounder*, which he scored.

*MAY 17, 1950*

**Bill Bruford**: Birmingham, England. Drummer and original member of **Yes** until 1972 when he joined **King Crimson**. He played in **Gong, Pavlov's Dog** and **Genesis** before emerging with a new version of King Crimson in 1981.

*MAY 18, 1949*

**Rick Wakeman**: West London, England. Keyboardist on sessions with **Cat Stevens, David Bowie** and **T. Rex** before joining **The Strawbs** in 1970 and **Yes** in 1971 as replacement for **Tony Kaye**. Wakeman's first solo LP, *The Six Wives of Henry VIII*, released while still a member of Yes, earned high critical praise. He interrupted a solo career to rejoin **Yes** in 1977, only to quit again in 1981.

*MAY 19, 1945*

**Pete Townshend**: London, England. Singer, guitarist and composer with **The Who**, a band that evolved from **The Detours** and **The High Numbers** in the early Sixties. Townshend, along with **Roger Daltrey, John Entwistle, Keith Moon** and **Kenney Jones**, has had a profound influence on rock both with The Who and through his solo compositions.

*MAY 19, 1952*

**Joey Ramone**: New York City. Singer and founding member of **The Ramones**.

*MAY 20, 1944*

**Joe Cocker**: Sheffield, England. Singer and drummer best known for his gutsy vocals and spastic gestures. Cocker rose to fame with **The Grease Band**, then with **Leon Russell** in the massive *Mad Dogs & Englishmen* tour. His solo career has been punctuated with bouts of alcoholism, but he marked a return in 1982 with a highly acclaimed LP, *Sheffield Steel*.

*MAY 20, 1946*

**Cher**, born Cherylyn Sakasian LaPierre: El Centro, California. Singer and songwriter who began as background vocalist with **Phil Spector** before marrying **Sonny Bono** and making hit history as **Sonny and Cher**. Her acting career includes a role in *Come Back to the Five and Dime, Jimmy Dean, Jimmy Dean*, both on stage and screen, and her supporting role in *Silkwood*, which won her a 1983 Academy Award nomination.

### MAY 21, 1948

**Leo Sayer**, born Gerard Sayer: Sussex, England. Singer and songwriter who began with early blues rockers **Alexis Korner, Mike Chapman** and **Mike Cooper** before fronting his own band, **Patches**, in 1972. He co-wrote songs for **Roger Daltrey**'s first solo LP before a successful solo career of his own.

### MAY 22, 1950

**Bernie Taupin:** Lincoln, England. Singer and songwriter who first teamed with **Elton John** in a talent competition in 1967 and went on to pen numerous hits in the Seventies including "Your Song," "Honky Cat" and "Goodbye Yellow Brick Road."

### MAY 23, 1934

**Robert Moog.** Inventor of the Moog Electronic Music Synthesizer, a staple of nearly all rock bands.

### MAY 24, 1941

**Bob Dylan**, born Robert Allen Zimmerman: Duluth, Minnesota. The birth of a legend! A man who singlehandedly diverted the course of modern music. While in college he takes a new name, Bob Dylan, in honor of a boyhood hero, Dylan Thomas, the poet. The early years as a musician are spent on the streets and in the coffeehouses of Greenwich Village, where he's discovered by Columbia Records executive, **John Hammond**, and records his first and most famous song, "Blowin' In the Wind." When Dylan decides to "go electric," folk fans agonize and desert him, only to become part of the legions of new converts who are drawn to "Like a Rolling Stone," "Lay Lady Lay" and later "Hurricane." Dylan's religious conversion to born again finds him recording Christian songs in the late Seventies, but his role in music is not diminished.

### MAY 25, 1926

**Miles Davis:** Alton, Illinois. Trumpeter and true pioneer of the jazz-rock fusion with over 40 LPs in his career.

### MAY 26, 1943

**Levon Helm:** Marvell, Arkansas. Drummer with **Ronnie Hawkins and the Hawks**, then with **The Band** until its demise in 1976. His solo work continues and his film credits include *Coal Miner's Daughter* and *The Right Stuff*.

### MAY 26, 1948

**Stevie Nicks**, born Stephanie Nicks. Singer and songwriter who teamed with **Lindsey Buckingham** in the early Seventies and later as a pair joined **Fleetwood Mac** at the invitation of **Mick Fleetwood**. A separate solo career has exploded Stevie Nicks to international stardom with the hits "Stop Dragging My Heart Around" and "Edge of Seventeen" while she continues recording with **Fleetwood Mac**.

*MAY 28, 1944*

**Gladys Knight**: Atlanta, Georgia. Singer and songwriter best known for her soul hits with **The Pips**.

*MAY 28, 1945*

**John Fogarty**: Berkeley, California. Guitarist and singer with **Creedence Clearwater Revival** until 1971, then with **The Blue Ridge Rangers**.

*MAY 31, 1938*

**Peter Yarrow**: New York City. Partner in the Sixties folk-pop **Peter, Paul and Mary**, famous for their versions of "Puff the Magic Dragon," "Blowin' in the Wind" and "Leaving on a Jet Plane."

*MAY 31, 1948*

**John "Bonzo" Bonham**: Worcestershire, England. Drummer with **Led Zeppelin**, creating the driving beat that helped push the band to the heights of rock fame. His death on September 25, 1980 led to the supergroup's disbanding.

*JUNE 1, 1947*

**Ron Wood**: Middlesex, England. Guitarist with early roots in **The Jeff Beck Group** and **The Faces**, then in 1975 with **The Rolling Stones** as replacement for **Mick Taylor**.

*JUNE 2, 1941*

**Charlie Watts**: London, England. Drummer and original member of **The Rolling Stones**.

*JUNE 3, 1946*

**Ian Hunter:** Shropshire, England. Singer, songwriter and guitarist with **Mott the Hoople** until 1974 when he and **Mick Ronson** formed **The Hunter-Ronson Band**. A successful solo career followed.

*JUNE 6, 1939*

**Gary U.S. Bonds**: Jacksonville, Florida. Singer and songwriter successful in the early Sixties with "New Orleans" and "Quarter to Three," then re-emerging in 1982 with help from **Bruce Springsteen** and **"Miami" Steve Van Zandt**.

*JUNE 7, 1946*

**Bill Kreutzman**: Palo Alto, California. Drummer and original member of **The Grateful Dead**.

*JUNE 8, 1944*

**Boz Scaggs**, born William Royce Scaggs: Ohio. Singer, songwriter and guitarist with **The Marksmen** with **Steve Miller** before going solo in Europe and recording the LP *Boz* in Sweden. Teams with Miller for two Steve Miller Band LPs in the mid-Sixties, then solo again with his *Silk Degrees* album boosting him to stardom in 1976.

### JUNE 8, 1950

**Alex Van Halen**: Netherlands. Drummer with **Van Halen**, a band formed with brother **Eddie** in 1976.

### JUNE 9, 1923

**Les Paul**, born Lester Polfus: Waukesha, Wisconsin. Legendary guitarist, best known for his partnership with his wife, **Mary Ford**, and his association with guitarist **Chet Atkins**. The Les Paul line of guitars he developed for Gibson Corporation are standard items in many studios and rock bands.

### JUNE 9, 1934

**Jackie Wilson:** Detroit, Michigan. Singer who dropped a promising career in boxing to replace **Clyde McPhatter** in **The Dominoes**, going solo four years later. On September 29, 1975 his career ends when a massive heart attack hits while performing on stage in Philadelphia. He is best known for his hit singles "Lonely Teardrops" and "Higher and Higher."

### JUNE 10, 1910

**Howlin' Wolf**, born Chester Burnett: West Point, Mississippi. Blues singer and harmonica player most responsible for the blues revival of the Sixties, including his work with **Eric Clapton, Steve Winwood** and **The Rolling Stones.**

### JUNE 12, 1951

**Bun E. Carlos**. Drummer with **Cheap Trick.**

### JUNE 15, 1941

**Harry Nilsson:** Brooklyn, New York. Singer and songwriter who broke into the music business with the name **Johnny Niles** in the early Sixties. As Nilsson he wrote songs for **The Monkees, The Yardbirds** and **Blood, Sweat & Tears**. Best known for "Everybody's Talking," the theme from *Midnight Cowboy*, "The Point," and his association and work with **John Lennon** and **Ringo Starr.**

### JUNE 16, 1942

**James Paul McCartney:** Liverpool, England. Successful enough to be called J.P.! Becomes a larger-than-life figure in contemporary music. McCartney, with **John Lennon, George Harrison** and **Ringo Starr**, become **The Beatles** in 1961 and the course of rock music is permanently altered. Paul bears responsibility for the breakup of The Beatles in 1970, after a decade of fabulous successes, including more Number 1 hit records than any other musical group. His post-Beatles career has been as solo artist, with **Wings**, with **Stevie Wonder**, and occasional interactions with the former Beatles. McCartney has grown to be a devoted family man and collector of other's works, particularly the publishing rights to most of **Buddy Holly**'s material.

*Paul McCartney*

*JUNE 19, 1942*

**Spanky McFarlane**, born Elaine McFarlane: Peoria, Illinois. Singer and songwriter for **Spanky and Our Gang**, in the mid-Sixties best known for the hits "Sunday Will Never Be the Same," and "Like to Get to Know You." In 1982 she accepts an invitation to join a reformed **Mamas and Papas**.

*JUNE 19, 1950*

**Ann Wilson:** Vancouver, British Columbia. Singer and founding member of **Heart**, which her sister **Nancy** joined shortly thereafter.

*JUNE 20, 1942*

**Brian Wilson:** Hawthorne, California. Singer, songwriter, keyboardist and arranger with his group **The Beach Boys**. His beginnings are with **Carl and the Passions**, then **Kenny and the Cadets** before reaching spectacular success with a string of surf songs and ballads in the Sixties with **The Beach Boys**.

*JUNE 20, 1924*

**Chet Atkins:** Lutrell, Tennessee. Premiere guitarist who began as a session player before landing a record contract in 1946. Respected and admired as one of the best guitarists ever.

*JUNE 21, 1944*

**Ray Davies:** London, England. Singer and guitarist, the founding member of **The Kinks** with brother **Dave**. The basic dirty two-note guitar hook that made a hit with "You Really Got Me" continues to be the trademark of the band.

*JUNE 22, 1944*

**Peter Asher:** London, England. Singer, songwriter and producer. Famous as half of **Peter and Gordon**, then as successful manager and producer for **James Taylor** and **Linda Ronstadt**.

*JUNE 22, 1948*

**Todd Rundgren:** Upper Darby, Pennsylvania. Singer, multi-instrumentalist and producer who began with the band **Woody's Truckstop**, then formed **The Nazz** in 1968. His considerable production credits include work with **Janis Joplin, Badfinger, Grand Funk Railroad** and others. He formed **Utopia** in 1974 and records with them in the Eighties.

*JUNE 24, 1944*

**Jeff Beck:** Surrey, England. Guitarist who replaced **Eric Clapton** in **The Yardbirds** before forming **The Jeff Beck Group** with **Rod Stewart** in 1967, then with **Beck, Bogart and Appice**. A solo LP *Blow by Blow* was recorded in 1975 and his collaborations include work with **Jan Hammer**.

*JUNE 24, 1947*

**Mick Fleetwood:** Cornwall, England. Drummer and co-founder of **Fleetwood Mac**, a group that derives its name from Fleetwood and the "Mc" of bassist **John McVie**.

### JUNE 25, 1945

**Carly Simon**: New York City. Singer and songwriter who helped form **The Simon Sisters** with sister **Lucy** in the early Sixties. A solo artist in the early Seventies with a number of duets with husband **James Taylor**.

### JUNE 30, 1943

**Flo Ballard**: Detroit, Michigan. Along with **Diana Ross** and **Mary Wilson**, she formed **The Supremes** in the late Fifties and produced some of the biggest hits of the Sixties. She died in poverty, never having received royalties for her work.

### JULY 1, 1946

**Debbie Harry**: New Jersey. Former model and Playboy bunny turned singer and mascot of **Blondie** in the late Seventies.

### JULY 4, 1952

**John Waite**: London, England. Bassist and vocalist, he founded **The Babys** in 1976 and released his first solo LP "Ignition" in 1982.

### JULY 5, 1944

**Robbie Robertson**, born Jamie Robertson: Toronto, Canada. Guitarist and founding member of **The Band**, turned movie actor and producer. Good friend of **Bob Dylan**.

### JULY 6, 1925

**Bill Haley**, born William Clifton Haley: Highland Park, Michigan. Released "Crazy Man Crazy," the first rock 'n' roll record to enter U.S. charts, in 1953, and the classic "Rock Around the Clock" in 1954. Haley is often credited with starting the rock 'n' roll movement.

### JULY 7, 1940

**Ringo Starr**, born Richard Starkey: Liverpool, England. Drummer for **The Beatles** after departure from **Rory Storme and the Hurricanes**. Has put out many solo LPs and ventured into the film business.

### JULY 10, 1947

**Arlo Guthrie**: New York City. Son of legendary folk singer, **Woody Guthrie**, best known for "Alice's Restaurant," the song and the movie.

### JULY 12, 1943

**Christine McVie**, born Christine Perfect: England. Singer and keyboardist, she joined **Fleetwood Mac**, her husband's group, after a limp solo start. Still with Fleetwood Mac, she has continued to work on her own endeavors.

### JULY 13, 1942

**Roger McGuinn**, born James Joseph McGuinn: Chicago, Illinois. Singer-guitarist who formed **The Byrds** in 1965.

*JULY 14, 1912*

**Woody Guthrie**, born Woodrow Wilson Guthrie: Okema, Oklahoma. A legendary folk singer, from his pen emerged numerous American classics including "This Land Is Your Land." He died October 3, 1967, of Huntington's chorea and is survived by his son **Arlo Guthrie**, who carries on the musical tradition.

*JULY 15, 1946*

**Linda Ronstadt**: Tucson, Arizona. Singer first with the **Stone Poneys**, she hit paydirt as a solo artist with hits like "You're No Good" and "That'll Be the Day." A lead role in *The Pirates of Penzance* on Broadway introduced her to the musical theater in 1980.

*JULY 18, 1939*

**Dion**, born Dion DiMucci: New York City. Teen idol-vocalist of **Dion and the Belmonts**, his hits include "Teenager in Love" and "Runaround Sue."

*JULY 18, 1942*

**Martha Reeves**: Detroit, Michigan. She joined Motown Records as a secretary and ended up earning them millions fronting **The Vandellas** and hits like "Heatwave," "Jimmy Mack" and "Dancing in the Streets."

*JULY 19, 1947*

**Brian May:** Middlesex, England. Guitarist with **Queen**.

*JULY 20, 1947*

**Carlos Santana**: Autlan, Mexico. The guitarist's own group, **Santana**, emerged in the San Francisco music explosion of the Sixties. Their Woodstock appearance brought them to the forefront of rock in 1969.

*JULY 20, 1955*

**Michael Anthony**: Bassist with **Van Halen**.

*JULY 22, 1947*

**Don Henley**: Linden, Texas. Drummer with **The Eagles** after backup with **Linda Ronstadt**.

*JULY 26, 1943*

**Mick Jagger**: Kent, England. After starting with **Alexis Korner's Blues Incorporated**, he co-founded **The Rolling Stones** in 1963. The group is second perhaps only to **The Beatles** for setting the pace of Sixties rock and twenty years later, is going as strong as ever.

*JULY 31, 1946*

**Bob Welch**: Los Angeles, California. A singer-guitarist, he joined **Fleetwood Mac** in 1971 and left to pursue solo ventures in 1975. Best known for "Sentimental Lady" and "Ebony Eyes."

**AUGUST 1, 1942**

**Jerry Garcia**: San Francisco, California. Guitarist and founder of **The Grateful Dead**.

**AUGUST 1, 1960**

**Joe Elliot**: Birmingham, England. Vocalist for **Def Leppard**.

**AUGUST 4, 1946**

**Maureen Cox Starkey**: First wife of **Beatles** drummer, **Ringo Starr**. The marriage lasted until July, 1975.

**AUGUST 5, 1947**

**Rick Derringer**, born Richard Zehringer: Celino, Ohio. Had an international hit at age 15 with **The McCoys** "Hang on Sloopy." Later joined **Johnny Winter**'s backup group, then **Edgar Winter's White Trash**, before becoming a solo artist and recording another hit "Rock and Roll Hoochie Coo."

**AUGUST 10, 1947**

**Ian Anderson**: Edinburgh, Scotland. Vocalist and flutist, he formed **Jethro Tull** from the ashes of **The John Evans Band** in 1968. A colorful and flamboyant front man.

**AUGUST 10, 1947**

**Ronnie Spector**, born Veronica Bennett: New York City. Singer-songwriter with **The Ronettes** when producer, **Phil Spector**, spotted them, made them hitmakers with "Be My Baby," and she married him.

**AUGUST 13, 1951**

**Dan Fogelberg**: Peoria, Illinois. Singer-songwriter of such critically acclaimed albums as *Souvenirs*, *Captured Angel*, and *Netherlands*.

**AUGUST 14, 1941**

**David Crosby**: Los Angeles, California. First with **The Byrds**, he left in 1968 to form **Crosby, Stills & Nash** with **Steve** and **Graham**. Several solo recordings.

**AUGUST 19, 1939**

**Ginger Baker**, born Peter Baker: London, England. One of rock's leading drummers of the Sixties and Seventies, best known for work in **Cream** and **Blind Faith**, and a somewhat less successful solo venture, **Ginger Baker's Airforce**.

**AUGUST 20, 1943**

**Isaac Hayes**: Covington, Tennessee. Sax and piano player-composer, he's best known for his score to the film *Shaft*.

**AUGUST 21, 1938**

**Kenny Rogers**: Houston, Texas. Early successes in **The New Christy Minstrels** and **The First Edition** led to a superstar country music career.

### AUGUST 21, 1944

**Jackie De Shannon**: Hazel, Kentucky. Singer-songwriter who's appeared with **James Brown** and **The Beatles**, she's best known for writing hits for others, including "Put a Little Love in Your Heart" and "Bette Davis Eyes."

### AUGUST 23, 1947

**Keith Moon**: London, England. Drummer with **The Who** whose sheer energy more than made up for a lack of technical proficiency. Keith died of a drug overdose in September, 1978.

### AUGUST 25, 1949

**Gene Simmons**: Haifa, Israel. Fire-breathing bassist with **Kiss**.

### AUGUST 29, 1958

**Michael Jackson**: Gary, Indiana. Youngest of the **Jackson Five**, he rises to stardom in the late Seventies as a solo artist. His 1983 release *Thriller* is the largest selling album in recording history. Touring with his brothers, the 1984 summer *Victory* tour is expected to gross $50 million.

### AUGUST 30, 1985

**John Phillips**: Parris Island, South Carolina. Singer and songwriter with **The Mamas and the Papas**, a group he re-formed in 1982 after a breakup of more than a decade.

### AUGUST 31, 1931

**Jerry Allison**: Hillsboro, Texas. Friend of **Buddy Holly** and member of **The Crickets**.

### AUGUST 31, 1945

**Van Morrison**: Belfast, Ireland. Singer, songwriter and multi-instrumentalist, Morrison had an early hit in the group **Them** with "Gloria" and several as a solo artist, including "Moon Dance."

### AUGUST 31, 1983

**Tyrone Wood**. Son of **Rolling Stone** guitarist **Ron Wood** and wife **Jo**.

### SEPTEMBER 1, 1946

**Barry Gibb**: Isle of Man, England. Singer and guitarist with **The Bee Gees**, married on his birthday in 1970 to Scottish beauty queen, **Linda Gray**.

### SEPTEMBER 2, 1983

**Amy Rachel Osbourne**. Daughter of **Ozzy Osbourne** and wife, **Sharon**.

### SEPTEMBER 6, 1947

**Roger Waters**: Cambridge, England. Bassist and founding member of **Pink Floyd**, major creative participant in the 1982 film, *Pink Floyd: The Wall*.

### SEPTEMBER 7, 1936
**Buddy Holly**, born Charles Hardin Holley: Lubbock, Texas. Legendary Fifties rock star who, in two years, created singles history with "That'll Be the Day," "Peggy Sue" and other hits.

### SEPTEMBER 8, 1946
**Freddie Mercury**, born Frederick Bulsara: Zanzibar. Lead singer with **Queen**.

### SEPTEMBER 9, 1941
**Otis Redding**: Macon, Georgia. Singer and songwriter famous for his soul-wrenching R&B hits, "Try a Little Tenderness" and "Sittin' on the Dock of the Bay."

### SEPTEMBER 9, 1946
**Billy Preston**: Houston, Texas. Keyboardist and singer with **Little Richard** in 1963, then featured soloist with various artists including **The Beatles** on "Get Back." Various solo recordings.

### SEPTEMBER 10, 1939
**Cynthia Lennon**: Blackpool, England. First wife of **John Lennon**.

### SEPTEMBER 16, 1925
**B.B. King**: Itta Bena, Mississippi. Blues singer and guitarist.

### SEPTEMBER 18, 1940
**Frankie Avalon**, born Francis Avallone: Philadelphia, Pennsylvania. Teen idol of the Fifties with various "beach party" film credits, best known for the hit "Venus."

### SEPTEMBER 19, 1934
**Brian Epstein**: Liverpool, England. Manager of **The Silver Beatles**, then **The Beatles**, **Gerry and the Pacemakers**, **The Cyrkle** and **Billy J. Kramer and the Dakotas**.

### SEPTEMBER 19, 1943
**"Mama" Cass Elliot**, born Naomi Cohen: Baltimore, Maryland. Singer with **The Mugwumps** in 1964, then an original member of **The Mamas and the Papas**, with a successful solo career beginning in 1968. Mama Cass died on July 29, 1974 of a heart attack in the London flat of **Harry Nilsson**.

*Van Morrison*

### SEPTEMBER 22, 1958
**Joan Jett**: Landsdowne, Pennsylvania. Singer and guitarist with **The Runaways** before success as a solo artist with "I Love Rock and Roll."

### SEPTEMBER 23, 1930
**Ray Charles**: Albany, Georgia. Singer and pianist blinded in early childhood, respected as one of the most influential black musicians in the last three decades. Best known for "Georgia on My Mind."

### SEPTEMBER 23, 1949
**Bruce Springsteen**: Freehold, New Jersey. Singer and songwriter most commonly revered as "The Boss" for his commanding style and charisma. A relative unknown until the mid-Seventies press campaign that brought him to the covers of *Newsweek* and *Time* and hailed Springsteen as "the next **Bob Dylan**."

### SEPTEMBER 24, 1941
**Linda McCartney**, born Linda Eastman: Scarsdale, New York. A freelance photographer, married to **Paul McCartney** in 1969 and has recorded and performed in concert with him since.

### SEPTEMBER 26, 1945
**Brian Ferry**: Duran, England. Keyboardist and singer with **Roxy Music** and various LPs.

### SEPTEMBER 26, 1948
**Olivia Newton-John**: Cambridge, England. Singer and songwriter who began at age 14 in the **Sol Four**, then a successful solo career and film roles in *Grease* and *Xanadu* and *Two of a Kind*.

### SEPTEMBER 27
**Meat Loaf**, born Marvin Lee Aday: Dallas, Texas. Singer who started with **The Amboy Dukes** before landing a role in *The Rocky Horror Picture Show*, where he met lyricist **Jim Steinman**. The pair were successful on Meat Loaf's debut LP *Bat Out of Hell*.

### SEPTEMBER 29, 1935
**Jerry Lee Lewis**: Ferriday, Louisiana. Singer and pianist known to millions as "The Killer," Lewis began recording in 1957 with a string of hits to follow, including "Great Balls of Fire" and "Whole Lotta Shakin' Going On." Lewis suffered a serious illness in 1981, but recovered and continues vigorous performances.

*Jerry Lee Lewis*

## OCTOBER 2, 1945
**Don McLean**: New Rochelle, New York. Singer and guitarist who received national acclaim in 1971 with the hit single "American Pie."

## OCTOBER 3, 1938
**Eddie Cochran**: Albert Lea, Minnesota. Singer and guitarist in the Fifties rock scene, best known for "Summertime Blues."

## OCTOBER 3, 1941
**Chubby Checker**, born Ernest Evans: Philadelphia, Pennsylvania. Singer noted for the international hit "The Twist."

## OCTOBER 3, 1947
**Lindsey Buckingham**: California. Guitarist and singer with **Fleetwood Mac** after a duo career with **Stevie Nicks**. His solo career blossomed in the early Eighties.

## OCTOBER 4, 1944
**Nona Hendryx**: Trenton, New Jersey. Singer with **The Del Capris** before joining **Patti LaBelle** in 1962.

## OCTOBER 5, 1943
**Steve Miller**: Dallas, Texas. Singer, songwriter and guitarist with a college band, **The Marksmen Combo**, before forming **The Steve Miller Blues Band** in 1966, followed by a successful solo career.

## OCTOBER 8, 1951
**Johnny Ramone**: New York City. Guitarist with **The Ramones**.

## OCTOBER 9, 1940
**John Winston Lennon**: Liverpool, England. Singer, songwriter, guitarist and producer who formed the legendary **Beatles** in 1962. Lennon continued to record after the group disbanded in 1970, but stopped in 1975 when he was granted permanent resident status in the U.S. after a grueling court battle. A revitalized career in music was ended in 1980 when Lennon was shot to death in front of his apartment building in Manhattan shortly after the release of his LP *Double Fantasy*.

## OCTOBER 9, 1944
**John Alex Entwistle**: London, England. Bassist and original member of the supergroup, **The Who**, with occasional solo projects.

## OCTOBER 9, 1948
**Jackson Browne**: Heidelberg, Germany. Singer, guitarist and songwriter with **The Nitty Gritty Dirt Band**, then a successful solo artist.

*OCTOBER 9, 1975*

**Sean Ono Lennon**: New York City. Son of **John** and **Yoko**, born the same date as his father.

*OCTOBER 10, 1955*

**David Lee Roth**. Lead singer with **Van Halen**.

*OCTOBER 11, 1948*

**Daryl Hall**: Philadelphia, Pennsylvania. Singer and keyboardist, founding member of **Hall & Oates**.

*OCTOBER 13, 1925*

**Lenny Bruce**: New York City. Counter-culture comedian whose style paved the way for comics **George Carlin**, **Richard Pryor** and others.

*OCTOBER 13, 1941*

**Paul Simon**: Newark, New Jersey. Singer, songwriter and multi-instrumentalist who teamed with **Art Garfunkel** to form **Tom and Jerry**, evolving into **Simon and Garfunkel**. He is noted for both his duo and solo work, particularly "Sounds of Silence" and "Mother and Child Reunion."

*OCTOBER 14, 1940*

**Cliff Richard**, born Harry Rodger Webb: Lucknow, India. Singer, guitarist and actor best known in the U.S. for "Devil Woman" and "Don't Turn Out the Light."

*OCTOBER 16, 1947*

**Bob Weir**: San Francisco, California. Guitarist and singer with **The Grateful Dead**, as well as founder of his own band **Bobby and the Midnights**. Born with a rare brain disorder, Weir cannot read, although he aspires to be a writer.

*OCTOBER 18, 1926*

**Chuck Berry**: San Jose, California. Legendary singer and guitarist noted as the inspiration for many contemporary guitarists. Berry rose to fame in the mid-Fifties with "Johnny B. Goode" and "Maybelline" and many of his classics have been covered by newer rock groups, including "Roll Over Beethoven" by **The Beatles** and **The Electric Light Orchestra**.

*OCTOBER 19, 1944*

**Peter Tosh**, born Peter McIntosh: Jamaica. Singer and guitarist original member of **Bob Marley's Wailers**. Solo career after 1975 with support from **Mick Jagger** and his Rolling Stones Records.

*Peter Tosh*

### OCTOBER 20, 1953
**Tom Petty**: Florida. Guitarist, singer and founder of **Tom Petty and the Heartbreakers**.

### OCTOBER 21, 1940
**Manfred Mann**, born Michael Leibowitz: Johannesburg, South Africa. Keyboardist and founding member of **The Mann-Hugg Band** in 1963, evolving into **Manfred Mann**.

### OCTOBER 21, 1942
**Elvin Bishop**: Tulsa, Oklahoma. Guitarist with **The Butterfield Blues Band** in the mid-Sixties, then a solo career marked by the hit "Fooled Around and Fell in Love."

### OCTOBER 24, 1930
**The Big Bopper**, born J.P. Richardson: Sabina, Texas. Singer and songwriter best known for "Chantilly Lace" in the mid-Fifties, before he died in a plane crash with **Buddy Holly** and **Richie Valens**.

### OCTOBER 24, 1941
**Bill Wyman**, born William Perks: Kent, England. Bassist and original member of **The Rolling Stones**, joining the group shortly after **Mick Jagger** and **Keith Richard** left **Blues Incorporated** to form **The Stones**. Wyman occasionally records solo, produced three LP's of his own by the early Eighties.

### OCTOBER 25, 1944
**Jon Anderson**: Lancashire, England. Singer and founding member of **Yes** until the demise of the supergroup in 1981. Then a solo career and collaborations with **Vangelis**. The supergroup has since re-formed with an album release in 1983.

### OCTOBER 28, 1936
**Charlie Daniels**: Wilmington, North Carolina. Singer, guitarist, fiddler and songwriter who began as a session player for **Bob Dylan**, **Pete Seeger**, **Ringo Starr** and others before recording his own material in the early Seventies. Best known for his 1980 hit "In America."

### OCTOBER 29, 1944
**Denny Laine**, born Brian Arthur Hines: New Jersey. Guitarist with **The Diplomats** in the early Sixties, then with **The Moody Blues** in 1964 and with **Wings** in 1971, pursuing a solo career in 1981.

### OCTOBER 30, 1939
**Grace Slick**: Chicago, Illinois. Lead singer with **The Great Society** before replacing **Signe Anderson** in **Jefferson Airplane** in 1966. She has engaged in various solo projects during her on-again off-again relationship with **Jefferson Airplane-Starship**.

### NOVEMBER 2, 1944
**Keith Emerson**: England. Keyboardist with **The Nice** before co-founding **Emerson, Lake & Palmer** in 1970.

### NOVEMBER 5, 1931
**Ike Turner**: Clarksdale, Mississippi. Singer, songwriter and multi-instrumentalist who formed **The Kings of Rhythm** and scored with the song "Rocket 88" before his long association with wife Tina (Annie Mae Bullock).

### NOVEMBER 5, 1941
**Art Garfunkel**: New York City. Singer who joined **Paul Simon** to form **Tom & Jerry**, evolving into **Simon & Garfunkel**. The combination brought international success in the Seventies; when the two split, Garfunkel turned his interests to a film career. They reunited in New York's Central Park in 1981 for a concert and album.

### NOVEMBER 5, 1947
**Peter Noone**: Manchester, England. Singer and guitarist leader of **Herman's Hermits** in the Sixties and then **The Tremblers** in 1980.

### NOVEMBER 6, 1948
**Glen Frey**: Detroit, Michigan. Guitarist, keyboardist and singer with **The Eagles**, before going solo in 1982 with debut LP *No Fun Aloud*.

### NOVEMBER 7, 1937
**Mary Travers**: Louisville, Kentucky. Singer and founding member of **Peter, Paul & Mary**.

### NOVEMBER 7, 1943
**Joni Mitchell**, born Roberta Joan Anderson: Alberta, Canada. Singer and songwriter who began in coffeehouses around Canada before recording her first LP in 1964. Her songs have been recorded by **Judy Collins**, **Tom Rush**, **CS&N** among others. "Big Yellow Taxi" and "Help Me" established Mitchell as a major recording artist in her own right.

### NOVEMBER 8, 1949
**Bonnie Raitt**: Los Angeles, California. Guitarist and singer with a country-blues background in the Sixties, then rock-pop solo work in the Eighties.

### NOVEMBER 10, 1948
**Greg Lake**: Bournemouth, England. Guitarist and singer, one of the founding members of **King Crimson**, then **Emerson, Lake & Palmer**, with a solo career in 1981.

### NOVEMBER 12, 1945
**Neil Young**: Toronto, Canada. Guitarist, singer and songwriter in the Canadian folk scene until he formed **The Buffalo Springfield** with **Steve Stills** in 1966,

*Joni Mitchell*

followed by a solo LP, his partnership with **Crosby, Stills & Nash**, then solo again.

## NOVEMBER 20, 1946

**Duane Allman**: Nashville, Tennessee. Guitarist and co-founder of **The Allman Brothers Band**.

## NOVEMBER 20, 1947

**Joe Walsh**: Cleveland, Ohio. Guitarist and singer, founding member of **The James Gang** in 1965, then formed **Barnstorm** before joining **The Eagles** in 1976, with solid contributions to their Grammy winning LP *Hotel California*. Walsh continues to record and perform solo.

## NOVEMBER 22, 1949

**Steve Van Zandt**. Guitarist and singer with **Bruce Springsteen's E Street Band**, known as "Miami" Steve.

## NOVEMBER 26, 1938

**Tina Turner**, born Annie Mae Bullock: Brownsville, Tennessee. Singer and songwriter with husband **Ike Turner**, best known for the hit "River Deep, Mountain High." Her film credits include "Acid Queen" in *Tommy*. She is still going strong in 1984 with her Top 10 hit "What's Love Got to Do with It."

## NOVEMBER 26, 1945

**John McVie**: England. Bassist and original member of **John Mayall's Bluesbreakers** before forming **Fleetwood Mac** with **Peter Green** in 1967.

## NOVEMBER 27, 1942

**Jimi Hendrix**, born Johnny Allen Hendrix: Seattle, Washington. Guitarist and singer. Perhaps the most innovative guitarist of rock as a completely free-form experimenter with his instrument. Beginning as a session musician with **James**

Brown, **The Isley Brothers** and **Little Richard**, he formed the **Jimi Hendrix Experience** in 1966 in London with a boost into stardom at the Monterey Pop Festival and Woodstock. His unique guitar style remains unmatched.

### NOVEMBER 28, 1929

**Berry Gordy, Jr.**: Detroit, Michigan. Songwriter and record company executive who wrote the million seller "Lonely Teardrops" for **Jackie Wilson** and "You Got What It Takes" for **Marv Johnson**. Formed Tamla Records with $700 loan, which evolved into Motown Records, the hugely successful label for **The Supremes, Stevie Wonder, Smokey Robinson** and scores of others.

### NOVEMBER 28, 1943

**Randy Newman**: Los Angeles, California. Singer, songwriter and pianist best known for his biting lyrics on songs like the hit "Short People." Scored the soundtrack for the 1981 film *Ragtime*, which won him an Academy Award nomination.

### NOVEMBER 29, 1933

**John Mayall**: Cheshire, England. Singer and multi-instrumentalist, recognized as the "grandfather" of the British rock movement with his **Bluesbreakers** band, which allowed many of the top rock musicians a place to begin.

### NOVEMBER 30, 1929

**Dick Clark**: New York City. Disc jockey, concert promoter, TV host and producer. Although not a musician himself, Clark helped the careers of many musicians and singers by inviting them to perform on his *American Bandstand* TV show, one of the longest running TV programs to date.

### DECEMBER 1, 1936

**Lou Rawls**: Chicago, Illinois. Singer and songwriter with a gospel background and credits with **Sam Cooke**; a successful solo career followed.

### DECEMBER 1, 1945

**Bette Midler**: Paterson, New Jersey. Singer and songwriter who began as an actress and quickly moved to a bawdy cabaret-style stage show following the release of her first LP in 1972. Her film credits include the lead role in *The Rose* and *Divine Madness*.

### DECEMBER 2, 1960

**Rick Savage**: Birmingham, England. Guitarist with **Def Leppard**, an original member of the band.

### DECEMBER 3, 1948

**Ozzy Osbourne**, born John Robert Osbourne: Birmingham, England. Singer and songwriter with **Earth**, which evolved into **Black Sabbath**. Ozzy left in 1980 to pursue a successful solo career.

### DECEMBER 4, 1944
**Dennis Wilson**: Hawthorne, California. Drummer and original member of **The Beach Boys**. Died in 1983.

### DECEMBER 5, 1935
**Little Richard**, born Richard Penniman: Macon, Georgia. Singer, songwriter and pianist; one of the early innovators of rock 'n' roll with a string of hits, including "Long Tall Sally," "Good Golly, Miss Molly" and "Tutti Frutti."

### DECEMBER 7, 1942
**Harry Chapin**: New York City. Singer and songwriter best known for his storytelling in songs like "Taxi" and "Cat's in the Cradle." Heavily involved in benefit work for World Hunger.

### DECEMBER 7, 1949
**Tom Waits**: Pomona, California. Singer and songwriter best known for his gravel-voiced, smokey-bar style songs.

### DECEMBER 8, 1943
**Jim Morrison**: Melbourne, Florida. Singer and songwriter, founding member of **The Doors**, one of the top bands of the Sixties with "Light My Fire" and "Riders on the Storm." **The Doors** surged into popularity again in the early Eighties ten years after the band's demise.

### DECEMBER 8, 1947
**Gregg Allman**: Nashville, Tennessee. Keyboardist and singer with **The Allman Brothers Band**, a founding member with his brother Duane.

### DECEMBER 9, 1943
**Rick Danko**: Ontario, Canada. Bassist with **The Hawks**, which evolved into **The Band**, later pursued a solo career with a film debut in *Cannery Row*, released in 1982.

### DECEMBER 11, 1944
**Brenda Lee**: Atlanta, Georgia. Singer best known for her 1961 hit, "I'm Sorry."

### DECEMBER 11, 1954
**Jermaine Jackson**: Gary, Indiana. Singer with **The Jackson Five**, then went on to pursue a solo career. In 1984, he joined his brothers for The Jacksons' Summer *Victory* tour, one of the most publicized and promoted concerts in history.

### DECEMBER 13, 1949
**Ted Nugent**: Detroit, Michigan. Guitarist and singer with **The Lourdes**, then co-founder of **The Amboy Dukes** before launching a successful solo career.

### DECEMBER 15, 1922
**Alan Freed**: Pennsylvania. Famous Fifties DJ who coined the phrase "rock 'n' roll" and whose career ended with payola scandals of 1960.

### DECEMBER 15, 1942
**Dave Clark**: Tottenham, England. Drummer and founder of **The Dave Clark Five**, a band formed to raise money for Clark's rugby team.

### DECEMBER 17, 1942
**Paul Butterfield**: Chicago, Illinois. Singer, pianist, harmonica player with an early history with **Howlin' Wolf**, **Magic Sam**, and **Little Walter** before forming his own **Butterfield Blues Band**.

### DECEMBER 18, 1943
**Keith Richards**: Kent, England. Guitarist and singer with **The Rolling Stones**, a founding member and co-author of most Stones tunes.

### DECEMBER 19, 1941
**Maurice White**: Chicago, Illinois. Singer, percussionist and producer with **Earth, Wind & Fire**, the founding member.

### DECEMBER 19, 1943
**Alvin Lee**: Nottingham, England. Guitarist with **Britain's Largest Sounding Trio** with **Leo Lyons** before forming **Ten Years After**, then **The Alvin Lee Band** in the Seventies.

### DECEMBER 20, 1947
**Peter Criss**: New York City. Drummer and original member of **Kiss** until his departure in 1980 to pursue a solo career.

### DECEMBER 21, 1940
**Frank Zappa**: Baltimore, Maryland. Singer, songwriter, multi-instrumentalist and producer, founding member of **The Mothers of Invention** in 1964. Noted for his avant-garde compositions with more than thirty LPs recorded and various film credits including *200 Motels*.

### DECEMBER 21, 1946
**Carl Wilson**: Hawthorne, California. Guitarist and original member of **The Beach Boys**.

### DECEMBER 22, 1949
**Robin** and **Maurice Gibb**: Isle of Man, England. With older brother **Barry**, they formed **The Blue Cats**, which evolved into **The Bee Gees** when the family moved to Australia in the late Fifties.

### DECEMBER 23, 1940

**Jorma Kaukonen**: Washington, D.C. Guitarist with the original **Jefferson Airplane**, then founding member of **Hot Tuna**.

### DECEMBER 26, 1940

**Phil Spector**: New York City. Songwriter and record producer for numerous artists including **The Teddybears** (his own group), **The Crystals**, **The Ronnettes**, **Elvis Presley** and **The Beatles**. Recognized for developing the "wall of sound" recording technique. Film credits include the role of a coke dealer in *Easy Rider*.

### DECEMBER 28, 1946

**Edgar Winter**: Beaumont, Texas. Guitarist with his brother, **Johnny**, in **Black Plague** before forming **White Trash**, then **The Edgar Winter Group**.

### DECEMBER 29, 1946

**Marianne Faithful**. English folksinger first recognized in 1964 with "Come and Stay with Me," followed by a highly publicized relationship with **Mick Jagger** and later, a renewed solo career in 1979.

### DECEMBER 30, 1928

**Bo Diddley**, born Otha Ellas Bates: McComb, Mississippi. Singer, songwriter and guitarist noted for his influence on **The Rolling Stones**, **The Who** and others. Legendary for his early rock stage style and guitar riffs.

### DECEMBER 30, 1942

**Michael Nesmith**: Dallas, Texas. Guitarist with **The Monkees** as an original member of the TV show, then pursued a solo career, including record producing on his own label and video production.

### DECEMBER 31, 1943

**John Denver**, born Henry John Deutschendorf: Roswell, New Mexico. Singer and guitarist with **The Chad Mitchell Trio** before a solo career in 1969, including numerous television specials and film credits.

*The Bee Gees*

# ROCK DEATHS

### JANUARY 4, 1976

Former **Beatles** bodyguard and road manager **Mal Evans** is shot to death by L.A. police after threatening his live-in companion with a rifle during an argument. The police say Evans turned the rifle on them when forced to surrender.

### JANUARY 13, 1979

**Donny Hathaway** dies in a fall from a fifteenth-floor room at New York's Essex House Hotel. The 33-year-old singer, composer and arranger was recording a second album with **Roberta Flack** earlier in the day. Police couldn't say whether Hathaway jumped or fell accidentally.

### JANUARY 16, 1972

**David Seville** dies in Beverly Hills, California, after many successes with **Alvin and The Chipmunks** novelty records of the early Sixties.

### JANUARY 16, 1975

**Paul Beaver** dies of a stroke in Los Angeles. The electronic synthesizer wizard has brought the Moog to popularity with **Beaver and Krause**, and used it effectively on film soundtracks for *The Graduate, Catch 22, Performance,* and *Rosemary's Baby.*

### JANUARY 20, 1965

**Alan Freed**, the father of rock radio DJs, dies in a Palm Springs hospital of uremia. He was one of the first to program black music for a white audience and even gave it a name, "rock 'n' roll," coined from the lyrics of a **Bill Haley** tune. After tremendous popularity in the Fifties, Freed is indicted for payola in 1960 and dies before he can answer charges of income tax evasion involving income from "commercial bribery."

**JANUARY 21, 1984**

**Jackie Wilson** finally dies after collapsing with a heart attack during a performance in New Jersey and remaining for months in a coma. Wilson, one of the great vocalists of all time, was famous for such songs as "Lonely Teardrops" and "Higher and Higher."

**JANUARY 23, 1978**

**Terry Kath**, guitarist with **Chicago**, accidentally kills himself with his own 9mm pistol during a party in Los Angeles. Kath tells witnesses the gun is empty as he puts it to his head and pulls the trigger.

**JANUARY 29, 1981**

*Creem* magazine publisher **Barry Kramer** is found dead in his Birmingham, Michigan, apartment at age 37.

**FEBRUARY 2, 1979**

**Sid Vicious** of **The Sex Pistols** dies of a heroin overdose in Greenwich Village, not far from the apartment where he allegedly murdered his girlfriend. The end of the 21-year-old punk star comes only a day after he's bailed out of Rikers Island Prison.

**FEBRUARY 3, 1959**

Rock legends **Buddy Holly, Richie Valens** and **The Big Bopper** (J.P. Richardson) die in a small plane crash outside Mason City, Iowa enroute to a concert date. Holly is only 22 years old.

**FEBRUARY 8, 1973**

**Max Yasgur** dies of a heart attack in Florida. His dairy farm in upstate New York became the concert site of the Woodstock celebration in 1969.

**FEBRUARY 9, 1981**

**Bill Haley** dies of a heart attack in Harlingen, Texas. Haley and his group, **The Comets**, carved out a niche in rock history with the song that would become the rock 'n' roll anthem "Rock Around the Clock."

**FEBRUARY 15, 1981**

**Mike Bloomfield** dies in his car in San Francisco. The blues guitarist came to national prominence in the mid-Sixties for performances with **Paul Butterfield** and **Bob Dylan**, then formed **The Electric Flag**. Best known for his *Super Session* LP recorded in 1968 with **Steve Stills** and **Al Kooper**.

**FEBRUARY 19, 1980**

**AC/DC** singer **Bon Scott** dies of alcohol poisoning in London.

**FEBRUARY 21, 1976**

**Florence Ballard** dies a pauper in Detroit at age 32. One of the **Supremes**, she quits the group in 1967 after a string of Number 1 hits. Ballard never received any royalties for her work.

### FEBRUARY 21, 1982
**Murray the K** dies of cancer in Los Angeles. The New York DJ, known for his close association with **The Beatles** during their early American tours.

### FEBRUARY 26, 1977
Bluesman **Booker T. Washington** ("Bukka" White) dies.

### FEBRUARY 28, 1974
Singer **Bobby Bloom** dies of self-inflicted gunshot wounds in a West Hollywood motel.

### MARCH 5, 1973
**Mike Jeffrey**, manager for **Jimi Hendrix**, dies in a plane crash in France.

### MARCH 5, 1982
**John Belushi** dies of respiratory failure at a rented bungalow in Los Angeles. A regular player on *The National Lampoon Radio Show* and later on *Saturday Night Live*, Belushi branched into film work on *Animal House, 1941, The Blues Brothers* and *Continental Divide*. His death attributed to a drug overdose.

### MARCH 8, 1973
**Ron "Pigpen" McKernan** dies of a stomach hemorrhage at his home in Corte Madera, California. The keyboard player, vocalist and founding member of **The Grateful Dead** is 27.

### MARCH 16, 1968
**Tammi Terrell** dies of a brain tumor. Best known for her duets with **Marvin Gaye**, the end is signaled some months earlier when she collapes into Gaye's arms during a concert.

### MARCH 19, 1976
**Paul Kossoff** dies of a heart attack in his sleep enroute to New York from Los Angeles. This is the guitarist's second "death" in a year, after doctors pronounce him clinically dead in 1975, when his heart fails for 35 minutes before he can be revived. His band **Free** split up after his death.

### MARCH 19, 1976
Former **Uriah Heep** bassist **Gary Thain** dies from a drug overdose in his apartment.

### MARCH 19, 1982
**Randy Rhodes**, lead guitarist for **Ozzy Osbourne**, is killed in a small plane crash near Orlando, Florida, when the plane swoops low and explodes in a grove of pine trees.

### MARCH 28, 1974

**Arthur "Big Boy" Cruddup** dies of a stroke in Virginia. The alleged "father of rock 'n' roll" composed many hits, including "That's Alright Mama," recorded by **Elvis Presley**.

### APRIL 1, 1984

**Marvin Gaye**, brilliant Motown recording artist, is shot and killed by his father in a family dispute in his home. Gaye was riding the crest of a comeback, having recorded "Sexual Healing," a major hit. Others included "I Heard It Through the Grapevine" and "Let's Get It On."

### APRIL 5, 1981

**Bob "The Bear" Hite** dies of a heart attack in Venice, California, after years as the lead singer of **Canned Heat**.

### APRIL 8, 1976

**Phil Ochs** hangs himself at his sister's home in Queens, New York. The folk singer and political activist best known for anti-Vietnam war anthem "I Ain't Marching Anymore" takes his life following a period of deep depression.

### APRIL 10, 1962

**Stu Sutcliffe**, the original bassist for **John Lennon's Silver Beatles**, dies of a brain hemorrhage in Hamburg, Germany.

### APRIL 17, 1960

**Eddie Cochran** dies and **Gene Vincent** seriously injured when Cochran's car blows a tire and crashes at Chippenham, England. The two Fifties rockers were in the midst of a major British tour.

### APRIL 17, 1974

**Vinnie Taylor**, guitarist for **Sha Na Na**, dies from a heroin overdose in a Charlottesville, Virginia hotel.

### APRIL 21, 1978

**Sandy Denny** dies of a brain hemorrhage after falling down a flight of stairs. Her days as lead singer for **Fairport Convention** were followed by a successful solo career in Britain.

### APRIL 23, 1975

Vocalist and guitarist for **Badfinger, Peter Ham**, hangs himself in the garage of his London home only days after quitting the successful group. Ham was presumably despondent and depressed over his financial problems.

### APRIL 25, 1974

**Pamela Morrison**, wife of the legendary singer for **The Doors**, dies of a heroin overdose.

*APRIL 27, 1972*

**Blue Oyster Cult** manager **Phil King** is murdered by a gambling partner in New York City.

*APRIL 28, 1980*

**Tommy Caldwell**, bassist for **The Marshall Tucker Band**, dies from head injuries received in a car crash near his hometown of Spartanburg, South Carolina.

*APRIL 30, 1968*

**Frankie Lymon** dies of a heroin overdose, ending a singing career which began at age 14 when he recorded "Why Do Fools Fall in Love."

*APRIL 30, 1983*

**Muddy Waters**, the electric blues guitarist, dies of a cardiac arrest in his home in Downer's Grove, Illinois. He was a great influence on such artists as **Eric Clapton** and **The Rolling Stones**.

*MAY 3, 1972*

**Stone the Crows** guitarist **Les Harvey** is electrocuted on stage in Swansea, Wales, when a poorly grounded microphone wire shorts out. Harvey is literally thrown into the air by the shock as his girlfriend and group vocalist, **Maggie Bell**, watches in horror.

*MAY 4, 1970*

Four students die in a barrage of gunfire from the National Guard rifles at **Kent State University** in Ohio. The incident inspires the **Crosby, Stills, Nash & Young** anti-war anthem "Ohio."

*MAY 8, 1974*

**Graham Bond**, a founding father of rock 'n' roll, dies under the wheel of a tube train at Finbury Park Station, London. The latter part of his career was marked by frequent depressions due to drug addiction and his obsession with the occult.

*MAY 8, 1982*

**Neil Bogart** dies of cancer at age 39. The effervescent record company executive created numerous trends in his roller-coaster career, from his productions of "bubblegum" hits to the development of Casablanca Records, where he was responsible for the "disco explosion" led by **Donna Summer** and **The Village People** and "theatre rock stars" **Kiss**. Bogart's Casablanca Filmworks produced *The Deep* and other movies, with his final venture, Boardwalk Entertainment, developing his songstress, **Joan Jett**.

*MAY 11, 1981*

**Bob Marley**, the "King of Jamaican Reggae," dies in his sleep just forty hours after entering a Miami hospital where he was being treated for lung, liver and brain cancer. Marley is responsible for bringing reggae music and the Rastafarian doctrine to all corners of the globe and is mourned by tens of thousands of followers in his homeland.

*The Pretenders*

### MAY 14, 1976
Singer **Keith Relf** of **The Yardbirds** fame is electrocuted at his West London home while tuning an electric guitar.

### MAY 23, 1963
Blues great **Elmore James** dies. The distinctive guitarist is a great influence on the music of **Eric Clapton** and **George Harrison**, among others.

### MAY 30, 1980
Bassist **Carl Radle** dies of chronic kidney ailment at his home near Tulsa, Oklahoma. Radle is best known for his work with **Eric Clapton** on *Derek and the Dominoes* and with **Joe Cocker** on the *Mad Dogs and Englishmen* tour.

### JUNE 3, 1969
**Diana Ross**'s two pet dogs are inadvertently poisoned by rat bait in a backstage dressing room in Philadelphia.

### JUNE 3, 1975
Rock journalist **Ralph Gleason** dies. He was a major contributor to *Rolling Stone* magazine and a myriad of rock publications.

### JUNE 13, 1972
Singer **Clyde McPhatter**, a former member of **The Drifters**, dies of a heart attack in Teaneck, New Jersey.

### JUNE 15, 1968
Jazz guitarist **Wes Montgomery** dies of a heart attack in Indianapolis at age 45. On the day of his death, Montgomery had three LP's on *Billboard*'s Hot 100 chart.

### JUNE 16, 1982
**James Honeyman-Scott**, lead guitarist and songwriter with **The Pretenders**, dies at a friend's apartment in London after a benefit concert performance, apparently of natural causes. He was 25 years old.

*JUNE 29, 1975*

Singer-songwriter **Tim Buckley** dies of a heroin-morphine overdose in a Los Angeles hospital. Ten days later a research assistant at U.C.L.A. is charged with second degree murder for furnishing Buckley with the drugs that caused his death.

*JUNE 29, 1979*

**Lowell George**, the prolific singer, songwriter, guitarist and founder of **Little Feat**, dies of a heart attack in Washington D.C. while touring with his own new group.

*JULY 3, 1969*

Guitarist **Brian Jones**, recently departed from **The Rolling Stones**, is found dead floating in the swimming pool of his home in Hartfield, England. Brian's is the first in an eerie chain of rock superstar deaths over the next two years, which include **Janis Joplin, Jimi Hendrix,** and **Jim Morrison**. Brian is buried six days later in his home town of Cheltenham Spa, England.

*JULY 3, 1971*

**Doors** singer **Jim Morrison** dies of a heart attack in the bath of his Paris home. Rumors run rampant of the actual circumstances of his death (mainly that Jim OD'd on drugs), but none is proved. Morrison is buried in a Paris cemetery under the epitaph "James Morrison, poet." Ten years later, former **Doors** players **Ray Manzarek, Robbie Krieger** and **John Densmore** join hundreds of fans in a graveside tribute to Morrison.

*JULY 12, 1979*

Singer-songwriter **Minnie Ripperton** dies of cancer in her husband's arms in Los Angeles. Minnie first grabbed the national limelight with her 1974 hit "Lovin' You."

*JULY 14, 1973*

Former **Byrds** guitarist **Clarence White** is killed when he's struck by an automobile near Lancaster, California. The 29-year-old guitarist is thrown seventy-five feet into the air by the impact.

*JULY 15, 1958*

**John Lennon**'s mother, **Julia**, is killed in an auto accident in Liverpool. The loss is expressed over and over in much of Lennon's music.

*Jim Morrison and the Doors*

*JULY 16, 1981*

**Harry Chapin** is killed in a car crash on New York's Long Island Expressway when his blue 1975 Volkswagen Rabbit is hit from behind by a tractor-trailer. Harry dies of a massive heart attack.

*JULY 17, 1959*

Blues singer **Billie Holiday** dies of a heroin overdose. Billy is hailed as perhaps the finest female blues singer ever.

*JULY 23, 1979*

Grateful Dead piano player, **Keith Godchaux**, 32, dies of head injuries sustained in an auto accident two days earlier in Marin County, California. Keith and his wife, **Donna**, both joined the Dead in 1971 at a time when **Ron McKernan** was seriously ill with liver cancer.

*JULY 24, 1972*

Drummer **Bobby Ramirez**, 23, of **White Trash** is killed in a bar brawl in Chicago. One of his three attackers turns himself over to the police and is charged with first-degree murder.

*JULY 26, 1977*

**Led Zeppelin**'s U.S. tour is abruptly halted when singer **Robert Plant** gets word from England that his six-year-old son, **Karac**, died. The boy was a victim of complications from a virus. The tour is never resumed.

*JULY 29, 1974*

**Cass Elliott** of **The Mamas and the Papas** dies of a heart attack in the London flat of Harry Nilsson. The 32-year-old singer is at first believed to have choked on a ham sandwich.

*AUGUST 1, 1964*

Singer **Johnny Burnette** ("You're Sixteen") dies at the height of his career in a boating accident in Clear Lake, near San Francisco, California.

*AUGUST 2, 1972*

**Brian Cole**, 28, one of the original members of **The Association**, dies in his Los Angeles home of a heroin overdose.

*AUGUST 8, 1975*

**Julian "Cannonball" Adderly**, saxophonist, famous for his 1965 Grammy Award winner "Mercy, Mercy, Mercy," dies of a stroke in Gary, Indiana.

*AUGUST 9, 1969*

Actress **Sharon Tate** and four others are victims in a bizarre night of murder. Charles Manson, who is charged and found guilty of the crime, claims **The Beatles** spoke to him through "secret messages" in the lyrics of five songs on the *White Album* and told him to do it.

### AUGUST 9, 1973

**Lillian Roxon**, author of the *Rock Encyclopedia*, dies of a severe asthma attack at age 41. The Australian-born writer was one of the world's premiere rock journalists, whose columns appeared regularly in *Mademoiselle, Oui,* and *The New York Sunday Times.*

### AUGUST 9, 1974

Trumpeter **Bill Chase**, 39, and three members of his group are killed in a plane crash in Jackson, Minnesota.

### AUGUST 12, 1975

Former **Who** manager **Pete Meaden** commits suicide.

### AUGUST 13, 1971

Soul saxophonist **King Curtis** is stabbed to death following an argument with an associate in front of his New York brownstone apartment.

### AUGUST 14, 1958

**Elvis Presley**'s mother, **Gladys**, dies in Memphis Methodist Hospital of a heart attack at age 42. Elvis is furloughed from his Army post in Fort Hood, Texas, to attend the funeral.

### AUGUST 16, 1977

Millions mourn the world over when **Elvis Presley**, the king of rock 'n' roll, dies at his Graceland mansion in Memphis, Tennessee, under confused and sordid circumstances. First reported to be a heart attack, it's later learned that his passing is almost certainly due to drug abuse. Elvis's personal physician is later found guilty of overprescribing medication to Elvis.

### AUGUST 17, 1973

**Paul Williams**, singer and arranger of the original **Temptations**, is found dead slumped over the steering wheel of his car in Detroit. He has a gun in his hand and a bullet in his head. The coroner rules suicide.

### AUGUST 18, 1977

Outside the gates of Graceland Mansion in Memphis, two young girls are killed and another seriously injured by a runaway car which strikes them as they pay final respects to their idol, **Elvis Presley.**

### AUGUST 27, 1967

**Beatles** manager **Brian Epstein** is found dead at his home in London from an accidental overdose of Carbitol, a sleeping pill. Stunned by the news, the four Beatles rush back from their visit with the **Maharishi Mahesh Yogi** in Bangor.

### SEPTEMBER 3, 1970

**Al Wilson** is found dead in the back of the home of fellow Canned Heat member, **Bob "The Bear" Hite**. Wilson, the band's guitarist, singer and harmonica player, is recognized as one of the world's foremost authorities on the blues.

### SEPTEMBER 6, 1978

**Tom Wilson** influential record producer of the Sixties, dies of a heart attack at his Los Angeles home at age 47. Wilson is best known for producing three early **Bob Dylan** LP's and the single "Like a Rolling Stone," **Simon & Garfunkel's** "Wednesday Morning, 3 a.m." and the *Freak Out* LP for **Frank Zappa and the Mothers of Invention.**

### SEPTEMBER 7, 1978

**Keith Moon** dies of a drug overdose in the bedroom of his London flat after attending the film premiere of *The Buddy Holly Story*. The legendary drummer with the **Who** was plagued by progressively failing health during the last years of his life, due to his quick-paced, overindulgent lifestyle.

### SEPTEMBER 16, 1977

**Marc Bolan,** the lead singer and founding member of **T. Rex** is killed when a car in which he's riding crashes into Barnes Bridge, London.

### SEPTEMBER 18, 1970

**Jimi Hendrix** dies of asphyxiation when he chokes on his own vomit after taking an overdose of sleeping pills in the apartment of girlfriend, **Monika Danneman. Eric Burdon,** with whom Jimi was visiting at the time, claims Hendrix left a suicide note, although it was never seen.

### SEPTEMBER 19, 1973

**Gram Parsons** of **The Flying Burrito Brothers** dies of multiple drug use while rehearsing in the desert outside Los Angeles. His coffin is stolen from the grave a week later and his body cremated at Joshua Tree National Monument, according to Parsons's wish as expressed to friend and road manager, **Phil Kaufman.**

### SEPTEMBER 20, 1973

**Jim Croce** dies with six others in a chartered plane that crashes on take-off at Natchitoches, Louisiana.

### SEPTEMBER 20, 1980

**Kathy Collins,** wife of **Rossington-Collins** founder, **Al Collins,** dies of a heart attack after an extremely difficult pregnancy. The band's tour is postponed.

### SEPTEMBER 23, 1974

**Average White Band** drummer **Robbie McIntosh** dies from a heroin overdose at a party in North Hollywood, apparently mistaking the heroin for cocaine.

### SEPTEMBER 25, 1980

**John Bonham** of **Led Zeppelin** dies at the home of guitarist **Jimmy Page** after a long night of heavy drinking. The coroner's report reveals Bonham has ingested 40 measures of vodka. His death means the end of the historic supergroup.

### SEPTEMBER 27, 1972

**Rory Storme** dies from an overdose of sleeping pills and his mother commits suicide on the same day. Storme was leader of **Rory Storme and The Hurricanes**, which featured **Ringo Starr** on the drums.

### SEPTEMBER 27, 1979

**Jimmy McCullough** is found dead in his flat in Maida Vale, England. Before joining and leaving **Paul McCartney**'s band, **Wings**, McCullough played with **Thunderclap Newman** and **Stone The Crows**.

### SEPTEMBER 29, 1975

**Jackie Wilson**'s career ends when he's struck with a massive heart attack while performing in Philadelphia. Neither the orchestra nor audience realize what is happening when the singer slumps to his knees during the concert.

### OCTOBER 1, 1975

**Al Jackson** of **Booker T. and The MG's** is shot dead in his East Memphis home by burglars. The drummer is 39.

### OCTOBER 3, 1967

**Woody Guthrie** dies of Huntington's Chorea, a rare hereditary disease, after nearly fifteen years of paralysis. The legendary folk singer wrote scores of great American standards including "This Land is Your Land" and influenced the styles of many folksingers who followed his career ... **Pete Seeger, Bob Dylan** and Woody's son, **Arlo**.

### OCTOBER 4, 1970

**Janis Joplin** dies of a heroin overdose in a Hollywood hotel room. Her talents were brought to national attention following her performance with **Big Brother and the Holding Company** at the Monterey Pop Festival. Her most successful LP *Pearl*, is released posthumously.

### OCTOBER 6, 1967

"Death of a Hippie" funeral service is held by **The Diggers** in Haight-Ashbury in San Francisco, as participants ceremoniously fill a coffin with stereotyped hippie artifacts and set it aflame to symbolize the end of the "media-hyped movement."

### OCTOBER 11, 1978

**Nancy Spungen** is found murdered in the bathroom of the Greenwich Village apartment she shared with boyfriend **Sid Vicious** of **The Sex Pistols**. Vicious is arrested a day later and charged with the stabbing death.

### OCTOBER 15, 1977

**Lynyrd Skynyrd**'s *Street Survivors* LP is released featuring an album cover showing group members enveloped in flames. The cover is changed when three members of the band are killed in a plane crash five days later.

### OCTOBER 16, 1969

**Leonard Chess** dies at age 52. The founder of Chess Records assured success for the label when he and his brothers signed **Chuck Berry**.

### OCTOBER 17, 1972
**Billy Williams** dies, best known for his hit "Write Myself a Letter."

### OCTOBER 18, 1974
Soul singer **Al Green** is scalded when his girlfriend, **Mary Woodson**, throws boiling grits at him before shooting herself. Green suffers severe burns on his back. His girlfriend dies instantly.

### OCTOBER 20, 1977
Three members of **Lynyrd Skynyrd** are killed when their tour plane crashes in Mississippi. Dead are lead singer **Ronnie Van Zandt**, guitarist **Steve Gaines**, and singer **Cassie Gaines**. The other band members who survive do not reform the group, even though it is on the verge of stardom, but choose to cast the survivors as **The Rossington-Collins Band**.

### OCTOBER 21, 1965
**Bill Black**, the original bassist with **Elvis Presley** and later of his own **Bill Black Combo**, dies in Memphis, Tennessee.

### OCTOBER 25, 1976
**Phillip Reed** dies in a fall from a Salt Lake City hotel room. Before joining **Flo and Eddie**, guitarist Reed is known as one of the best session players in Los Angeles.

### OCTOBER 29, 1971
**Duane Allman** dies in a motorcycle crash on a winding road near Macon, Georgia. The leader and guitarist with **The Allman Brothers Band** is just 24 years old.

### OCTOBER 31, 1956
**Mary Patricia McCartney**, mother of **Paul McCartney**, dies in Liverpool.

### NOVEMBER 5, 1960
**Johnny Horton** dies in a car crash near Milano, Texas, as his career is in full stride from the 1959 hit "Battle of New Orleans."

### NOVEMBER 5, 1977
**Guy Lombardo** dies of a heart attack in Houston, Texas, where his band was performing, forever ending a standard tradition of **Guy Lombardo and the Royal Canadians** bringing in the new year.

### NOVEMBER 6, 1972
New York Dolls drummer **Billy Muncia** dies of accidental suffocation when a girl pours coffee down his throat after he nods off in her apartment following a night at the London Speakeasy Club. Muncia is 21.

### NOVEMBER 11, 1972
**Barry Oakley**, bassist with **The Allman Brothers Band**, dies when his motorcy-

cle slams into a bus in Macon, Georgia, just three blocks from the site where Duane Allman lost his life in a similar mishap a year before. Oakley is 24.

### NOVEMBER 17, 1979
**John Glascock**, bassist with **Jethro Tull**, dies at age 27 in London following open heart surgery.

### NOVEMBER 18, 1971
**Junior Parker** dies during an eye operation, leaving behind a history of famous recordings, including "Bad Woman, Bad Whiskey."

### NOVEMBER 18, 1972
**Danny Whitten**, singer and songwriter with **Crazy Horse**, dies of an accidental drug overdose at the home of a friend.

### NOVEMBER 20, 1973
Comedian **Alan Sherman** dies of respiratory failure. The Jewish comedian established his popularity in the Sixties with the novelty hit, "Hello Mudda, Hello Fadda."

### DECEMBER 1, 1969
**Magic Sam** dies at age 32. He's a blues guitarist and singer best known for the 1964 hit "High Heeled Sneakers."

### DECEMBER 3, 1979
Eleven concert-goers die and dozens are injured during the rush to get good seats at a **Who** concert in Cincinnati. Festival seating and too few open doors are blamed for the tragedy and as a result, festival seating is banned in Cincinnati and other cities.

### DECEMBER 4, 1976
Guitarist **Tommy Bolin** dies of a heroin overdose in a Miami hotel.

### DECEMBER 6, 1969
Four die at a **Rolling Stones** concert at Altamont Speedway near San Francisco, including 18-year-old Meredith Hunter who is stabbed to death by a Hell's Angel security guard. Both the concert and murder are captured in the film *Gimme Shelter,* which premieres in New York exactly one year later.

### DECEMBER 8, 1980
**John Lennon** is shot and killed outside the Dakota Apartments in New York City after he and Yoko return from a recording session for their next album. Murderer Mark David Chapman fires the four shots at Lennon after calling out his name.

### DECEMBER 10, 1967
**Otis Redding** and four of the **Bar-Kays** are killed in a plane crash near Madison, Wisconsin.

### DECEMBER 10, 1976
Guitarist **Tommy Bolin** is buried wearing the same ring worn by **Jimi Hendrix** the day he died, a present from **Deep Purple**'s manager.

### DECEMBER 11, 1964
**Sam Cooke** is shot and killed under sordid circumstances by a 22-year-old woman he allegedly was trying to rape. A court later ruled the shooting was justifiable homicide in self defense. Cooke was 34.

### DECEMBER 20, 1973
**Bobby Darin** dies of a heart attack in a Los Angeles hospital at age 37 during his second open heart operation in two years.

### DECEMBER 25, 1954
Singer **Johnny Ace** shoots himself in a game of Russian roulette backstage at City Auditorium in Houston, Texas.

### DECEMBER 27, 1976
Blues great **Freddie King** dies after becoming ill at a Christmas Day concert in Dallas, Texas.

### DECEMBER 28, 1983
**Beach Boys** drummer, **Dennis Wilson,** dies in a drowning accident while under the influence of alcohol and drugs, in Marina Del Rey, California.

### DECEMBER 29, 1980
**Tim Hardin** is found dead in his Hollywood apartment from a heroin overdose. The prolific singer-songwriter rose to prominence with such songs as "If I Were a Carpenter" and "Reason to Believe." He was 40.

*John Lennon and Yoko Ono*

# MARRIAGE & DIVORCE

### JANUARY 4, 1978
**Fleetwood Mac**'s original leader and founder **Peter Green** marries **Jane Samuel** in Los Angeles.

### JANUARY 9, 1973
**Lou Reed** marries a New York City cocktail waitress named **Betty**.

### JANUARY 9, 1977
**Emmylou Harris** marries **Brian Ahern**, her producer, in Halifax, Nova Scotia.

### JANUARY 16, 1979
The divorce is finalized for **Cher** and **Gregg Allman**, four years after papers were filed. Cher filed them nine days after the wedding.

### JANUARY 21, 1966
Tears everywhere as **Beatle George Harrison** weds actress **Patricia Boyd** after a brief courtship. Patti played one of the schoolgirls in the train scene near the start of the film *A Hard Day's Night,* the production which brought the two together.

### JANUARY 23, 1979
**Brian Wilson** of **The Beach Boys** is divorced from his wife of fifteen years, **Marilyn Rovell**. She was just sixteen years old when they wed.

### JANUARY 26, 1970
**Jefferson Airplane** drummer **Spencer Dryden** marries **Sally Mann**.

### JANUARY 28, 1968
**Roger Daltry** is sued for divorce by his wife of four years, **Jacqueline**.

### FEBRUARY 4, 1974
**John** and **Yoko** split up, the relationship strained from their immigration ordeal.

### FEBRUARY 11, 1965
**Ringo Starr** marries **Maureen Cox** in London. It lasts ten years.

### FEBRUARY 16, 1963
**Paul Anka** marries **Ann Dezogheb** in Paris.

**FEBRUARY 20, 1974**
**Cher** files for separation after ten years of marriage to **Sonny Bono**.

**FEBRUARY 20, 1982**
**Pat Benatar** marries guitarist-producer **Neil Geraldo** on the Hawaiian island of Maui. This just four days before winning her second Grammy.

**MARCH 1, 1977**
**Sara Dylan** files for divorce after twelve years of marriage to **Bob Dylan**.

**MARCH 1, 1980**
**Patti Smith** marries **Fred Smith**, former **MC5** guitarist, in a civil ceremony in Detroit. The bride wears ballet slippers.

**MARCH 5, 1975**
**Rod Stewart** and **Britt Ekland** begin a highly publicized romance after meeting at a party given by **Joni Mitchell** in Los Angeles.

**MARCH 12, 1969**
**Paul McCartney** marries freelance photographer, **Linda Eastman**, in a small civil ceremony in London. The wedding news is all but overshadowed by another **Beatle** event that same day.

**MARCH 24, 1984**
**Al Jardine** of **The Beach Boys** marries **Mary Ann Helmandollar** in Scottsdale, Arizona.

**MARCH 28, 1979**
**Eric Clapton** marries **Patti Boyd**, former wife of **George Harrison**, in Tucson, Arizona. Clapton says Patti inspired him to write "Layla."

**APRIL 6, 1979**
**Rod Stewart** and **Alana Hamilton** are married in the Beverly Hills home of **Tina Sinatra**.

*Rod Stewart*

*APRIL 10, 1981*

**Pretenders** guitarist **James Honeyman-Scott** marries model **Peggy Sue Fender** in London.

*APRIL 11, 1981*

Guitarist **Eddie Van Halen** marries actress **Valerie Bertinelli** of television's *One Day at a Time*.

*APRIL 27, 1981*

**Ringo Starr** marries actress **Barbara Bach** at London's Marylbone Registry Office. The **McCartneys, George Harrison** and **Harry Nilsson** are in attendance.

*MAY 1, 1967*

**Elvis Presley** marries **Priscilla Beaulieu**, his long-time sweetheart, at The Aladdin Hotel in Las Vegas. The wedding cake alone cost $3,500.

*MAY 5, 1984*

**Chrissie Hynde** of **The Pretenders**, marries **Jim Kerr** of **Simple Minds** after a long relationship with **Ray Davies** of **The Kinks**, the father of her child.

*MAY 12, 1971*

**Mick Jagger** marries **Bianca Perez Morena de Macias** in a Roman Catholic ceremony in St. Tropez. The British press has a field day reminding the world of Jagger's "bad boy" image, particularly on the occasion of a full-blown church wedding to a woman of social stature and grace.

*MAY 16, 1981*

**Martin Chambers** of **The Pretenders** marries **Tracy Atkinson** in Los Angeles.

*MAY 21, 1968*

**Pete Townshend** marries **Karen Astley**, a dress designer who created some of the more outlandish outfits in the later Sixties.

*MAY 21, 1983*

**Michael MacDonald**, ex-**Doobie Brother**, marries singer **Amy Holland**.

*JUNE 11, 1983*

**Alex Van Halen** marries **Valeri Kendall**.

### JUNE 23, 1967
**Who** bassist **John Entwistle** marries **Alison Wise**. "I suspected we would marry. I was already playing in an amateur group and on our first date, Alison carried my amplifier."

### JUNE 26, 1975
**Sonny** and **Cher**'s divorce is finalized, leaving her free to marry guitarist **Gregg Allman** of **The Allman Brothers**, which she does four days later.

### JUNE 30, 1975
**Cher** marries **Gregg Allman**. The marriage will last only ten days.

### JULY 1, 1968
**John Lennon** publicly announces his love for **Yoko Ono** at the opening of his first art exhibition in London.

### JULY 1, 1975
**Ringo Starr** and wife **Maureen** divorce.

### JULY 3, 1960
**Elvis Presley** is heartbroken when father, **Vernon**, announces his plans to marry **Dee Alliot**, less than two years after his mother's death.

### JULY 10, 1975
**Cher** files for divorce from **Gregg Allman**. She accused him of moonlighting with an old flame.

### JULY 27, 1972
**Tony Banks**, keyboardist of **Genesis**, marries in Farnham, Surrey, England. All Genesis members, former and present, are on hand.

### AUGUST 7, 1974
**Peter Wolf** of the **J. Geils Band** marries actress **Faye Dunaway** in Beverly Hills after dating for almost a year.

### AUGUST 16, 1983
**Paul Simon**, one half of **Simon & Garfunkel** and composer of such great songs as "Bridge Over Troubled Water," "Still Crazy After All These Years," "Late in the Evening," marries **Carrie Fisher**, Princess Leia of *Star Wars* fame. They separate less than a year later.

### AUGUST 19, 1973
Singers **Kris Kristofferson** and **Rita Coolidge** marry in Los Angeles.

### AUGUST 23, 1962
**John Lennon** marries art student **Cynthia Powell**, at Mount Pleasant Registry Office in Liverpool, with **Paul McCartney** as best man.

### SEPTEMBER 18, 1969
**Tiny Tim** announces his engagement to **Miss Vicki Budinger** at the New Jersey State Fair. The wedding is to be telecast nationwide on *The Tonight Show* with Johnny Carson.

### OCTOBER 9, 1973
**Elvis** and **Priscilla Presley** are divorced in Santa Monica, California. Priscilla is awarded a generous settlement of nearly $1.5 million cash, $4,200 a month alimony for one year, half the sale price of the couple's $750,000 home and a 5% interest in two of Elvis's publishing companies.

### OCTOBER 14, 1964
**Charlie Watts**, drummer with **The Rolling Stones**, marries **Shirley Ann Shephard** in Bradford, England.

### OCTOBER 17, 1975
**Maurice Gibb** of **The Bee Gees** marries former restaurant manager **Yvonne Spencely**, a woman he met shortly after being separated from his first wife, British pop singer **Lulu**.

### OCTOBER 28, 1968
**Cynthia Lennon** sues **John Lennon** for divorce on grounds of adultery, a charge John doesn't defend because **Yoko** is pregnant with his child at the time.

### OCTOBER 31, 1970
**Michele Phillips**, formerly with **The Mamas and the Papas**, marries actor **Dennis Hopper**, star of *Easy Rider*.

### NOVEMBER 3, 1972
**James Taylor** and **Carly Simon** are married in her Manhattan apartment at 6:30 PM. With the exception of **Liz** and **Dick**, the couple are said to be the highest paid married couple in the world and on the eve of the marriage, Carly takes a bow with James at his concert at Radio City Music Hall.

### NOVEMBER 8, 1968
**John** and **Cynthia Lennon**'s divorce is final.

### NOVEMBER 22, 1965
**Bob Dylan** and **Sara Lowndes** are married. He described her as the "sad-eyed lady of the lowlands."

### DECEMBER 2, 1979
**Kris Kristofferson** and **Rita Coolidge** divorce after six years of marriage, a time during which each has built a successful career. The two appeared together in the film *Pat Garrett and Billy the Kid*.

## DECEMBER 3, 1938
**Alfred Lennon** and **Julia Stanley** marry. They have one child, a son, **John**.

## DECEMBER 10, 1968
**Robin Gibb** of **The Bee Gees** marries **Molly Hullis** after two years of living together.

*Robin Gibb and wife, Molly*

## DECEMBER 12, 1957
**Jerry Lee Lewis** secretly marries 13-year-old **Myra Lewis**, the daughter of his cousin, **J.W. Brown**. The marriage takes place a full five months before Lewis is divorced from his second wife and is such a major scandal that it nearly ruins his career.

## DECEMBER 18, 1983
**Keith Richards** ends months of speculation and marries model **Patti Hansen** in Mexico.

## DECEMBER 18, 1969
**Tiny Tim** marries **Miss Vicky** on *The Tonight Show*. Tiny is 40, Miss Vicky just 17.

## DECEMBER 29, 1975
**Grace Slick** and **Paul Kantner** call it quits after living together for seven years. Though they never married, they have a daughter, **China**, and shortly after the separation, Grace marries **Jefferson Starship** lighting director **Skip Johnson**.

# TOP 25
## rock & roll single artists

- CHUCK BERRY
- DAVID BOWIE
- JAMES BROWN
- RAY CHARLES
- ERIC CLAPTON
- ELVIS COSTELLO
- BOB DYLAN
- ARETHA FRANKLIN
- JIMI HENDRIX
- BUDDY HOLLY
- MICHAEL JACKSON
- BILLY JOEL
- ELTON JOHN
- JANIS JOPLIN
- CAROLE KING
- JOHN LENNON
- JERRY LEE LEWIS
- PAUL McCARTNEY
- ELVIS PRESLEY
- LOU REED
- DIANA ROSS
- BRUCE SPRINGSTEEN
- STEVIE WONDER
- NEIL YOUNG
- FRANK ZAPPA

*Chuck Berry*

*Elton John*

*Bruce Springsteen*

# TOP 25
## rock & roll bands

- THE BAND
- BEACH BOYS
- BEATLES
- CLASH
- CROSBY, STILLS, NASH, YOUNG
- DOORS
- EAGLES
- EVERLY BROTHERS
- FLEETWOOD MAC
- GENESIS
- GRATEFUL DEAD
- JACKSON FIVE
- KINKS
- LED ZEPPELIN
- PINK FLOYD
- POLICE
- PRETENDERS
- QUEEN
- ROLLING STONES
- SIMON & GARFUNKEL
- TALKING HEADS
- TEMPTATIONS
- VAN HALEN
- WHO
- YES

*The Everly Brothers*

*The Jacksons*

*Pretenders*

# *foreign bands and artists*

## (excluding U.K./U.S.)

- **ABBA** (Swed.)
- **AIR SUPPLY** (Aust.)
- **BOB MARLEY & THE WAILERS** (Jam.)
- **EDDY GRANT** (Bahamas)
- **FALCO** (Vien.)
- **GRACE JONES** (Jam.)
- **JOAN ARMATRADING** (St. Kitts)
- **KRAFTWERK** (Germ.)
- **LITTLE RIVER BAND** (Aust.)
- **LOVERBOY** (Can.)
- **MEN AT WORK** (Aust.)
- **MEN WITHOUT HATS** (Can.)
- **MENUDO** (P.R.)
- **NEIL YOUNG** (Can.)
- **NENA** (West Germ.)
- **NINA HAGEN** (East Germ.)
- **PETER TOSH** (Jam.)
- **PLASTIC BERTRAND** (France)
- **STRANGLERS** (Br/Swed/France)
- **YELLOWMAN** (Jam.)

*Bob Marley*

*Kraftwerk*

# bands of the eighties

*Psychedelic Furs*

- SIMPLE MINDS
- THOMPSON TWINS
- BAUHAUS
- THE CRAMPS
- SIOUXSIE & THE BANSHEES
- PETER GABRIEL
- STRAY CATS
- MADONNA
- BILLY IDOL
- CULTURE CLUB
- EURYTHMICS
- GRAND MASTER FLASH
- NINA HAGEN
- PSYCHEDELIC FURS
- ENGLISH BEAT
- SPARKS
- LORDS OF THE NEW CHURCH
- THOMAS DOLBY
- THE CURE
- BIG COUNTRY
- X
- THE FIXX
- BLASTERS
- BELLESTARS
- BAD BRAINS
- LENE LOVICH
- STYLE COUNCIL
- PETE SHELLEY
- RICHARD HELL
- U2
- PiL
- PRINCE
- SPANDAU BALLET
- MISSING PERSONS
- HUEY LEWIS & THE NEWS
- BRYAN ADAMS
- BANANARAMA
- CYNDI LAUPER
- QUIET RIOT
- R.E.M.
- INXS
- DURAN DURAN
- MADNESS
- DEF LEPPARD
- MOTLEY CRUE
- XTC
- NEW ORDER
- UB40

*Madonna*

# ELVIS
## the final summer

It was June 21, 1977, and it was muggy in Rapid City, South Dakota. A documentary crew had been feverishly busy all day getting footage of Elvis fans for a special preface to the live performance. Elvis's staunchest and most adoring loyalists would declare their undying love and explain why they had come all the way from such and such a small town in the Midwest just to be at the concert ("I have my little daughter with me," explained one lady fan, "and I've *always* talked about how great he was when I was growing up so she had no idea who he is! And a kid just can't grow up not knowing Elvis, is how I feel! He is *just* the King! He will *always* be the King no matter what...").

Elvis was standing off to the side in the right wing before he would make a specially designated entrance for the cameramen, dressed and ready to go as usual, garbed that night in a yellowish-beige jumpsuit with a golden sun rising in relief on his chest in an Inca mosaic of precious stones and golden thread, the gold-fringed collar in matching pattern and the gold-studded belt hung tightly on his waist, centered by an enormous rectangular buckle. The same gold-encrusted design adorned the sharply flared pantlegs all the way down to the white patent leather boots.

The Boss seemed completely absorbed as Rick stood by him, the light from the stage dancing off the Martin guitar that hung off Elvis's shoulder. His hair was sprayed and combed back carefully, his chin encroached down into his collar. Everything seemed ready to go, but it seemed somehow different that night because Elvis had too much on his mind. Rick knew that the cameras were making the difference.

It was the first time that Elvis would be in front of cameras of *any* kind in quite some time. The criticism of the tours during the previous year churned in his mind ("His attempts to perpetuate his mystique of sex and power end in weak self-parody," *Variety* had pronounced. "Elvis is neither looking or sounding good. He's thirty pounds overweight: he's puffy, white-faced, and blinking against the lights"), and what seemed strange as they stood there was that the cameras — friends to Elvis's career for so long — now seemed like cold intruders, even adversaries.

Elvis was tired, troubled, ravaged by drugs, and grossly overweight; he looked terrible, and he knew it. For the first time in his life he had to step out to public scrutiny without the benefit of his good appearance, knowing that the cameras would unsympathetically reflect all that had happened to him and all that he had become. He felt naked.

The band broke into the rumbling barrage of drums that led into *Also sprach Zarathustra* and the introductory strains of "See See Rider" and "That's All Right (Mama)." Rick again glanced at the Boss: He had that faraway, lost look of a man pondering his life and staring into the abyss of himself, when the images and events of a life all seem to blow through a mind at once. Rick had seen that look before, when Elvis would wax philosophical about something. Still, he wondered what was tumbling through Elvis's mind...probably Gladys...Cilla and Lisa...Linda...Daddy being so sick...the bad articles...now Red and Sonny were writing that book about him. He knew how tired Elvis was as the Boss licked his parched lips, took a deep breath, and steadied himself.

Elvis frowned sadly and turned to him. "Know what, Rick? I may not look too good for my television special tonight, but I'll look good in my coffin."

And with that, Elvis Presley stepped out to face America for the last time.

The bright lights of Memphis twinkled in the distance and the Mississippi snaked sluggishly off into nothingness as the roller coaster climbed to a dazzling height with a jerking motion. Preparing himself for the adventure, Rick turned to wink at Elvis, who sat in the car behind him smiling with his arm around Lisa.

Lisa knew something was up because Rick and Elvis always acted like a couple of idiots to make her laugh when they took her out to Libertyland. Rick stood and perched himself on the side of his car and at the split second as the train paused before it dipped, he wailed like a banshee into the night and leapt through the air to clutch onto the rafters and side railing where he hung like a monkey to enjoy Lisa gasping and Elvis roaring with laughter. He stood there chuckling as the train disappeared down the tracks, shaking the rafters and trailing away in Lisa's long and delightful scream. When the train came round again, Rick popped back into his car and Lisa looked reproachfully at him and said, "Ricky, don't *do* that!" before they plunged again. Then they got on the Dodge 'Em bumper cars and rode for what seemed like hours before dawn, when they got back in the car to head home.

Lisa was enjoying her several weeks visiting her daddy and granddaddy at Graceland before returning to Los Angeles to start school. The weather in Memphis that August had been tropical in humidity, blistering under a Southern sun that hung day after day in the sky to scorch the city, turning the poorer sections into an inferno and making it so hot that you couldn't even go outside without sweating clear through your shirt in a matter of minutes.

Elvis had returned from his last tour to spend the final few weeks of Lisa's summer vacation at Graceland and was gearing up for an eleven-day tour slated to begin on the sixteenth, when he would fly off to do a show in Portland, Oregon, and finish with two successive shows back in Memphis at the Mid-South Coliseum on the twenty-seventh and twenty-eighth. As usual he avoided the heat, preferring the air-conditioned and dehumidified atmosphere of his bedroom during the day and the cool of the night, when he would take Lisa out to Libertyland for excursions on Casey's Cannonball and the Little Dipper.

The usual contingent was there at Graceland getting ready for the tour — Charlie, Ricky, David, Dick, Billy Smith — with the other principals expected to arrive in town by the sixteenth for the tour. Ginger Alden was spending her nights with Elvis at Graceland and David and Rick were on duty as usual, alternating their nights and days on call for the Boss. Joe Esposito, who usually arrived in town a day or two before the tour to put things in order, was in town by the fifteenth. Things were progressing. Taking care of business as usual.

The Boss got up late the afternoon of the fifteenth and David then came by to talk to Elvis about his impending divorce. He was depressed about Angie, and Elvis counseled him to remain strong and keep on pushing despite his vanishing hopes for a reconciliation. David left and tried to psych himself up for the tour. At nightfall Elvis took Ginger out for a ride in his Stutz and then returned to relax and put some of his affairs in order before the tour.

Anyone passing the mansion on the night of the fifteenth or the early morning hours of the sixteenth would have seen the light burning brightly on the second floor where Elvis stayed. Rick was on duty and he was busy getting Elvis's trunks ready before David was scheduled to come on duty at noon. Rick hadn't had a chance to get his own clothes washed, folded and packed for the tour, so he was planning to double back to his apartment when David came on. He was no longer seeing Jill, but they were still good friends and she would give him a hand.

Sometime around 2:00 a.m., Elvis wanted to play racketball. Though terribly out of shape, he had been doing a little swimming and racketball to limber up for the tour and that way avoid muscle pulls on stage when he moved. The court, which Elvis had built when he became a racketball enthusiast, is located at the right side of the house, in the left part of the backyard, and Elvis, Ricky, Ginger, Billy Smith, and his wife, Josie, accompanied him down there. In sneakers, shorts, and sweat shirts, Elvis, Rick and Billy smacked the ball against the wall for some two hours. "Elvis didn't get out there and bust it," Rick remembers, "but he played. It didn't seem that he was over-exerting himself or anything like that."

Rick stayed with Elvis until five or six that morning, when Elvis handed him a prescription for Dilaudid. Rick went out and had it filled quickly. The drug was in capsule form and Rick noted that the dosage was no more than usual, certainly not enough to cause any undue concern on his part. "It wasn't any amount that could have even come close to killing him," he says flatly, "but if he had been straight when he had the heart problem, who knows man, he might have survived."

Rick and Elvis spent some time alone after Billy Smith left and Ginger was out of the room. Elvis was in the mood to pray. Rick was one of the few people that Elvis showed his spiritual side to, and when the mood struck him, they often prayed together. That year, with his knowledge and anxieties about Red and Sonny's book, they prayed more often than ever before. Around six o'clock they sat on Elvis's bed, clasped their hands together, and closed their eyes.

"Lord," Elvis prayed aloud, "help me to have insight and forgive me for my sins. Let the people who read that book have compassion and understanding about the things I've done. Dear God, please help me to get back when I feel down like this, and to always strive for good in the world. In the name of Jesus Christ, Amen."

Rick nodded his "amen" to Elvis.

"Ricky, tell David when he comes on tomorrow not to disturb me under any circumstances," the Boss said. "I don't want to get up until about four. Need plenty of rest for the tour."

"Okay," Rick said. "I'll start gettin' the rest of your stuff down and I'll see you later."

"Good night, Rick."

"Sleep well, Elvis," he said, closing the door quietly.

The morning air was still outside as the sun began to poke its head over that part of the world, sending low, mellow rays over Graceland and casting the estate in summer dawn tones. The horizon was tint-edged a beautiful orange-red; birds chirped peacefully as Elvis slept and nothing disturbed the tranquility of the morning save a random car or two passing the mansion on Elvis Presley Boulevard.

Inside the mansion, silence also reigned. Elvis and Ginger were asleep in his bedroom and Lisa slept in her bedroom upstairs. Aunt Delta was asleep downstairs in her bedroom; so was Minnie Mae Presley. Vernon and Sandy Miller slumbered in the house on Dolan where Dee Presley had raised her boys.

The others on the grounds also slept soundly, Charlie Hodge in the furnished apartment above the garage and Billy Smith with his family in their trailer quarters. Joe Esposito was in his room at the Howard Johnson's Motor Lodge in Whitehaven. The only people awake were Pauline Nicholson, Elvis's trusted housekeeper, Harold Lloyd, who manned the front gate, and Rick, who busied himself with various chores and waited for his brother David. He would remember to pass on the message about Elvis wanting to sleep for as long as possible.

Elvis woke up sometime around nine o'clock. It was not unusual for him to rise after only several hours sleep (even with the sleeping medication) and sometimes take more medication to get back to bed; other times, he felt like staying up and reading or watching television. These were the moments when the TCB boys would have to be most on their toes in case Elvis needed them or something was to go wrong. If a woman was sleeping with him, they were always instructed to call if anything unusual happened, unless it was Linda Thompson, who was always on top of the situation. Ginger had learned the score, but that morning, after Elvis told her that he was going to his bathroom, she dropped back to sleep. Considering her scant three hours of sleep and that she was anyway probably not fully awake in the darkness created by Elvis's specially lined dark curtains, it isn't hard to understand why.

Located off his bedroom on the second floor was Elvis's outsized and luxurious bathroom. With its walls knocked out to create space, Elvis had transformed it into a combination bathroom-office-study-lounge. One wall is mirrored and fringed with those large, spare lightbulbs that one usually associates with the dressing room of a star. Under the mirror is a large Formica table top with a sunken purple sink upon which were strewn all of Elvis's toilet articles. The shower, a circular one with its walls done in a brown, black and white tile design, is situated right next to the counter. The room is carpeted in plush purple; books, comfortable easy chairs, a television and other items of leisure are placed casually about.

The Boss's bathroom was the most private room in the house and the most private place in his life. Nobody ever went in without knocking. It was logical that the most private sanctuary in a life so fraught with publicity would have to be the bathroom, so Elvis made it into the place where he could be alone with his thoughts and most intimate with himself. The distance from the bathroom door (a heavy wooden one) to the bed where Ginger slept is approximately thirty feet.

Very few people know *exactly* what happened next, and that's probably the way Elvis would have wanted it. It is known that he sat on a chair and read for a while, and David would later recall that it was *Shroud of Turin* by Ian Wilson, a book about Jesus and the evolution of Christian theology that Larry Geller had given Elvis as a present. It is also known that sometime between ten and two-thirty that afternoon, Elvis had a heart attack. The preliminary findings by Dr. Jerry Francisco, the Shelby County coroner, would rule that cardiac arrhythmia and hardening of the arteries were the "natural" causes of death. Elvis may or may not have taken more of his sleeping medication; he may or may not have taken a dangerous amount of that medication if he did take more. If he had taken more and then had his coronary difficulty, the narcotics, as Rick suggested, may very well have impaired his ability to react and help himself. If he experienced a serious heart failure with an acute chest pain such as that felt during a massive heart attack, he couldn't have lasted for more than three to five minutes, in which case the narcotics would have lessened the pain considerably.

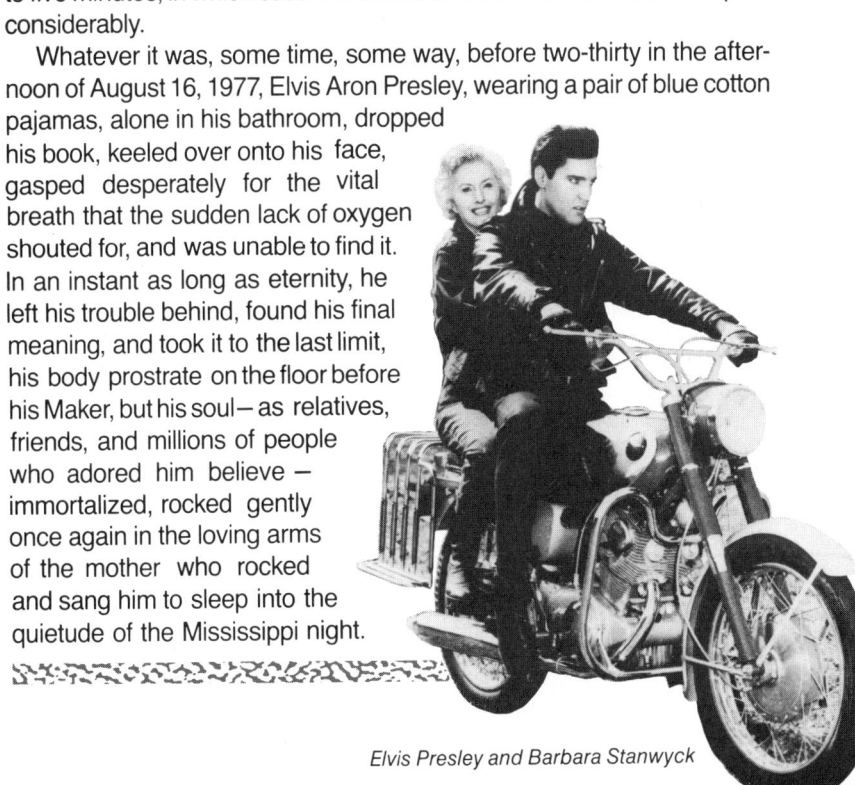

Whatever it was, some time, some way, before two-thirty in the afternoon of August 16, 1977, Elvis Aron Presley, wearing a pair of blue cotton pajamas, alone in his bathroom, dropped his book, keeled over onto his face, gasped desperately for the vital breath that the sudden lack of oxygen shouted for, and was unable to find it. In an instant as long as eternity, he left his trouble behind, found his final meaning, and took it to the last limit, his body prostrate on the floor before his Maker, but his soul — as relatives, friends, and millions of people who adored him believe — immortalized, rocked gently once again in the loving arms of the mother who rocked and sang him to sleep into the quietude of the Mississippi night.

*Elvis Presley and Barbara Stanwyck*

# Bad News Blues

*JANUARY 16, 1980*

**Paul McCartney** is busted by customs officials at Tokyo International Airport when nearly a half-pound of pot is discovered in his suitcase. The former Beatle is detained for nine days before being kicked out of Japan.

*JANUARY 18, 1980*

**Plasmatics** lead singer **Wendy O. Williams** is allegedly fondled and beaten by Milwaukee police as they arrest her after a **Plasmatics** concert. Williams is charged with "simulating masturbation on stage."

*JANUARY 30, 1974*

**Greg Lake** is arrested for skinny-dipping in a Salt Lake City hotel pool, clearly visible from the street.

*JANUARY 31, 1970*

**Bob Weir** and **Phil Lesh** of **The Grateful Dead** are busted along with 17 others after a Dead concert in New Orleans. Group members claim it was all a set-up.

*FEBRUARY 12, 1967*

**Keith Richards, Mick Jagger** and **Marianne Faithful** are busted for drug possession at Keith's home in West Wittering, England, the first of a highly publicized chain of drug busts involving **The Rolling Stones** members.

*FEBRUARY 15, 1976*

**Bette Midler** bails out seven members of her entourage following a bust for cocaine and pot possession.

*FEBRUARY 20, 1976*

Pharmacist **Joe Fuchs**, pleads guilty to conspiracy for the sale of drugs to **Gregg Allman** via group roadie **Scooter Herring**.

### FEBRUARY 22, 1980

**Rolling Stone** guitarist **Ron Wood** and a girlfriend are arrested in St. Maarten when police find five grams of cocaine in the couple's rented apartment. No charges are filed.

### FEBRUARY 27, 1970

**Jefferson Airplane** is fined $1,000 for singing the "ultimate" profanity while on stage in Oklahoma City. City fathers enforce the ordinance prohibiting obscene language on stage, drawn up a year earlier when **Doors** singer, **Jim Morrison**, fondled himself at a Miami concert date.

### FEBRUARY 27, 1977

**Keith Richards** is busted in a Toronto hotel by Canadian Mounties who uncover one ounce of heroin. The sentence Keith draws is to include a benefit **Rolling Stones** concert.

### FEBRUARY 28, 1972

The **"French Connection"** drug bust occurs at the port of Marseilles, as authorities seize 937 pounds of pure heroin valued at $100 million.

### MARCH 1, 1969

**Jim Morrison** is arrested during a concert at the Dinner Key Auditorium in Miami, charged with lewd and lascivious behaviour, open profanity, indecent exposure and public drunkenness. "It was real hot, and Jim was real drunk, but as far as I can see he didn't drop his pants." – **John Densmore, Doors** drummer

### MARCH 2, 1975

**Linda McCartney** is busted when Los Angeles police stop the car carrying Linda

*Ron Wood*

and Paul and catch a whiff of marijuana. A quick search yields eight ounces of pot in Linda's purse.

## MARCH 4, 1970
**Janis Joplin** is fined $200 and court costs for using obscene language on stage in Tampa, Florida.

## MARCH 8, 1973
**Paul McCartney** is busted for growing pot on his farm in Campbelton, Scotland.

## MARCH 12, 1969
**George Harrison** and his wife **Patti** are arrested at their home and are charged with possession of 120 joints of marijuana. Harrison claims "frame-up" and says the raid is timed to coincide with Paul's wedding.

## MARCH 18, 1965
**The Rolling Stones** earn their "bad boys" reputation when the group members are fined five pounds each for urinating in front of a public filling station after a concert in Essex.

## MARCH 18, 1970
**Country Joe McDonald** is convicted of obscenity for leading his famous **"Fish"** cheer during a Worcester, Massachusetts concert. "Gimme an F...Gimme a U...Gimme a C...!"

## MARCH 20, 1968
**Eric Clapton, Neil Young, Richie Furay** and **Jim Messina** are arrested at a private home in Los Angeles and charged with "being in a place where it is suspected that marijuana is being used."

## MARCH 21, 1976
**David Bowie** and **Iggy Pop** are busted in a hotel room in Rochester, New York, and charged with possession of six ounces of pot.

## MARCH 27, 1973
**Jerry Garcia** of **The Grateful Dead** is busted for speeding on the New Jersey Turnpike, but the $15 dollar speeding ticket turns into $2,000 bail when the police find pot, cocaine and LSD in Garcia's car. He spends three hours in jail.

## MARCH 28, 1982
**David Crosby** is busted for possession of Quaaludes and drug paraphernalia, driving under the influence of cocaine and carrying a concealed .45 caliber pistol. Crosby replied when asked why carrying the pistol— "**John Lennon.**"

## APRIL 13, 1982
**David Crosby** is arrested on drug and weapons charges for the second time in two weeks when the police find the singer "preparing" cocaine in his dressing room, a pistol stashed nearby.

## APRIL 20, 1981
**John Phillips** is jailed after pleading guilty to charges of pill pushing. The judge suspends all but 30 days of his sentence and orders the founder of **The Mamas and The Papas** to join a drug abuse program and perform 250 hours of community service. Phillips later reforms the group with original **Denny Doherty** and new "Mamas" **Spanky McFarlane** and **McKenzie Phillips**, John's daughter.

## APRIL 26, 1982
**Rod Stewart** is mugged and robbed of his $50,000 Porsche by a gunman in broad daylight while Rod is walking his three-year-old daughter on Sunset Boulevard in Hollywood.

## APRIL 27, 1975
Five-hundred-and-eleven pot smokers are busted over the course of a five-night series of concerts by **Pink Floyd** at the sports arena in Los Angeles. The concert promoters accuse the LAPD of harassment.

## APRIL 27, 1976
**David Bowie**'s collection of Nazi books and momentos is confiscated by guards at the Russian-Poland border. Bowie tells customs officials that Britain would benefit from a fascist leader.

## APRIL 30, 1970
**Twiggs Lyndon**, road manager for **The Allman Brothers**, is booked on murder charges after the stabbing death of a New York nightclub owner.

## MAY 3, 1969
**Jimi Hendrix** is busted by Canadian Mounties at Toronto International Airport when they find several ounces of heroin in a travel bag.

## MAY 10, 1967
**Mick Jagger, Keith Richards** and **Brian Jones** are all defending themselves in separate drug-related cases.

## MAY 16, 1969
**Pete Townshend** spends a night in jail in New York City for assaulting a man at the Fillmore East. What Townshend didn't know was that the man who jumped on the stage during a **Who** set was a plainclothes policeman trying to grab Townshend's microphone to warn the audience that a fire had broken out.

## MAY 16, 1980
**Dr. George Nickopoulas** is indicted on fourteen counts of over-prescribing drugs to **Elvis Presley, Jerry Lee Lewis** and nine others.

## MAY 19, 1976
**Keith Richards** is busted when he slams his car into the center divider on a highway 60 miles north of London and police discover a silver cylinder containing cocaine.

*MAY 20, 1975*

Drug possession charges against **Linda McCartney** are dropped, but a Los Angeles court directs her to attend drug counseling, write an essay on the evil of drugs and asks her to promise not to get busted again. At least not in L.A.

*MAY 24, 1968*

**Mick Jagger** and **Marianne Faithful** are busted for drug possession at their London home on the same day "Jumpin' Jack Flash" is released by **The Rolling Stones.**

*MAY 27, 1977*

**Tom Waits** and a friend are arrested at a local coffee shop in Los Angeles for allegedly "disturbing the peace."

*MAY 30, 1971*

Many unhappy memories for many who attend a **Grateful Dead** concert in San Francisco when members of the band are accused of distributing LSD-laced apple juice to an unwitting audience. Police shut down the show and rush three dozen people to a nearby crisis clinic for treatment.

*JULY 13, 1972*

Sixty people are arrested and a dozen others injured when the crowd gets out of hand at a **Rolling Stones** concert in San Diego, California.

*JUNE 16, 1982*

Guitarist and singer **Donny Van Zant** of **.38 Special** is arrested on stage after a concert in Tulsa, Oklahoma, for public drinking in a dry town.

*JUNE 29, 1967*

**Mick Jagger** and **Keith Richards** are both found guilty on drug charges stemming from a February 27, 1967 bust at Keith's home in West Wittering, England. Mick is sentenced to three months in jail and is sent to Brixton Prison. Keith is sentenced to a year. Fans are shocked and outraged.

*JULY 3, 1975*

**Chuck Negron**, lead singer of **Three Dog Night**, is busted for drug possession in Louisville when police find a leather pouch with two grams of heroin and a gram of cocaine in his hotel room.

*JULY 4, 1972*

Sixty-one fans are arrested when **The Rolling Stones** play Washington D.C.

*JULY 6, 1980*

Thirty-six are arrested at a **Ted Nugent** concert in Hollywood, Florida, for pot-smoking, bottle-throwing and other offenses.

*Jim Morrison*

*JULY 7, 1975*
**Stones** guitarist **Keith Richards** is arrested in Arkansas and charged with possession of an offensive weapon and reckless driving.

*JULY 17, 1972*
**Sly Stone** is mistakenly arrested by overzealous police in Santa Monica for possession of dangerous drugs. Charges are dropped when the "dangerous drugs" turn out to be cold capsules.

*JULY 19, 1976*
**Allman Brothers Band** roadie, **Scooter Herring**, is sentenced to 75 years in prison for distributing cocaine and other narcotics to **Gregg Allman**. Gregg was granted immunity in exchange for his testimony.

*JULY 31, 1967*
**Mick Jagger** and **Keith Richards** are released from jail after spending a month behind bars for possession of dangerous drugs. Public outcry over their imprisonment succeeds in overturning Keith's conviction completely, while Mick is given a conditional discharge.

*JULY 31, 1980*
**John Phillips** of **The Mamas and the Papas** is arrested at his summer home in Water Mill, Long Island, as a principle in a major pill-pushing ring. John, known to have been a long-time cocaine addict, is later found guilty of the crime.

*AUGUST 4, 1970*
**Jim Morrison** is arrested and charged with public drunkenness in Los Angeles when he falls stone cold asleep on an old woman's front porch.

*AUGUST 10, 1972*
**Paul** and **Linda McCartney** are accused of drug possession by authorities in Sweden.

*AUGUST 14, 1970*
**Steve Stills** is arrested in a motel room in La Jolla, California, for possession of cocaine and barbiturates. When police are summoned by the motel manager, Stills is found crawling in the hallways.

### AUGUST 15, 1976
Violence and arrests plague the concert scene. In Detroit, racial violence prompts the arrests of 47 at an **Average White Band** concert... in Los Angeles 188 are arrested, mostly for drug possession, at a **Jethro Tull** concert at the Coliseum ... and in San Francisco, it took the combined efforts of 17 police departments to quell a bottle-throwing melee involving some 300 angry **ZZ Top** fans who couldn't get tickets.

### AUGUST 21, 1972
Police mace **Grace Slick** and manhandle **Paul Kantner** in an after-concert scuffle in Akron, Ohio. **The Jefferson Airplane**'s equipment manager, **Chick Casedy**, started the whole mess when he called the police "pigs."

### AUGUST 31, 1970
**Peter Yarrow** of **Peter, Paul, & Mary** is arrested for taking "immoral liberties" with a 14-year-old girl.

### SEPTEMBER 13, 1975
Atlanta vice squad officers bust members of **Dr. Hook** after finding an ounce of pot in one of their hotel rooms.

### SEPTEMBER 17, 1979
**Keith Richards**'s trial on heroin trafficking charges ends in Toronto.

### SEPTEMBER 20, 1970
**Jim Morrison** is found "not guilty" of lewd and lascivious behaviour for the pants-dropping scene during a concert in Miami. He is "guilty" of indecent exposure and profanity in a decision handed down by a Miami judge.

### SEPTEMBER 20, 1972
**Paul McCartney** is busted for growing pot on his farm in Scotland, the first of three famous pot busts.

### SEPTEMBER 25, 1979
**Elton John**'s manager is charged with assault and battery for hitting a doorman with a cane at San Francisco's Fairmont Hotel as he and Elton leave for the airport. **John Reid** is sentenced to work in a crime diversion program.

### SEPTEMBER 26, 1968
**Brian Jones** is fined $150 plus court costs after a judge finds **The Rolling Stones** guitarist guilty of possession of marijuana.

### OCTOBER 2, 1968
**The Grateful Dead** band members, **Bob Weir** and **Ron "Pigpen" McKernan**, are busted on a variety of drug charges when San Francisco police raid the group's Haight-Ashbury home armed with warrants, guns... and reporters.

### OCTOBER 14, 1972

**Joe Cocker** and six members of his band and road crew are busted for drug possession after a concert in Adelaide, Australia.

### OCTOBER 15, 1973

**Keith Richards** and **Anita Pallenberg** are busted for drug possession in Nice, France.

### OCTOBER 18, 1968

**John Lennon** and **Yoko Ono** are busted at **Ringo Starr**'s basement apartment in London's Montague Square for possession of cannabis resin. John pleads guilty so police won't press charges against Yoko, though he swears the hashish has been planted in the flat by police. The arrest becomes the backbone of the U.S. Immigration Department case to keep Lennon from becoming a U.S. citizen.

### OCTOBER 18, 1969

**Paul Kantner** is busted in Honolulu and charged with possession of marijuana after police catch **Jefferson Airplane** guitarist crawling through bushes outside his home with a joint clenched between his teeth. Kantner denied the police report and claims he was set up.

### OCTOBER 24, 1978

**Keith Richards** is found guilty of heroin possession by a Toronto judge, but is given a suspended sentence and one-year probation. The verdict comes one year and a half after Canadian Mounties found 22 grams of heroin in Keith's hotel room. The court's leniency is severely criticized.

### OCTOBER 31, 1967

**Brian Jones** of **The Rolling Stones** is sentenced to nine months in jail on drug charges and is released on bail.

### NOVEMBER 11, 1969

**Doors** singer **Jim Morrison** is arrested for "interfering with the flight of an international aircraft and public drunkenness."

*The Rolling Stones*

### NOVEMBER 15, 1969

**Janis Joplin** is busted for using "vulgar and indecent" language on stage in Tampa, Florida, and for allegedly threatening to kick a policeman in the face.

### NOVEMBER 21, 1980

**Eagles** drummer **Don Henley** is arrested at his home in Los Angeles when a 16-year old girl is found nude and overdosed on the premises. Henley is charged with possession of various drugs and contributing to the delinquency of a minor.

### NOVEMBER 23, 1979

**Marianne Faithful** is arrested at Oslo Airport and charged with possession of marijuana. She signs a full confession and is set free to resume her concert tour.

### NOVEMBER 30, 1973

Jazz drummer **Buddy Rich** is busted for possession of marijuana while touring Australia, the second bust of the 56-year-old percussionist. Rich pleads not guilty and charges are dropped.

### DECEMBER 1, 1976

**The Sex Pistols** shock Britain when the group leader, **Johnny Rotten**, swears on live TV. The network later determines that host, Bill Grundy, provoked the obscenities, but the group's fate is sealed. For days the British newspapers play up the event with headlines like "The Punks...Rotten and Proud of It," and many concert dates are cancelled on their first British tour.

### DECEMBER 3, 1976

A tired and punchy **Jackson Browne** drops his pants on stage at the Oakland Paramount Theater in California when a fan shouts to him "get loose!"

### DECEMBER 7, 1978

**Sid Vicious** is arrested for assaulting **Patti Smith**'s brother, **Todd**, with a beer mug in a Manhattan night club. Vicious was free on bail and awaiting trial for the murder of his girlfriend, **Nancy Spungen**.

### DECEMBER 19, 1969

**Mick Jagger** is busted for pot possession in London. He's fined 200 pounds sterling and sent on his way.

### DECEMBER 23, 1980

**John McVie** and wife, **Julie**, are busted at their resort home in Honolulu and charged with possession of cocaine when a drug sniffing dog alerts police to the contents of a package addressed to the McVies.

### DECEMBER 24, 1972

**Tom Johnston** of **The Doobie Brothers** is arrested for possession of marijuana in Visalia, California. In the spirit of Christmas, police release him in his own custody.

# WALK RIGHT BACK:
## the Everly Brothers Reunion

*Nashville... Summer 1983*

On a small rehearsal stage not far from the Grand Ole Opry House, two brothers fine-tune a number for an upcoming concert. To hear them, you'd never guess that a decade has passed since their last tour together. Their voices slip and slide around the melodies with effortless grace, and as instrumentalists, their craft is untarnished. The Everly Brothers gave rock 'n' roll a sense of romance, and their sweet, lilting harmonies, charged with a dose of countrified rock, sound better than ever.

The reunion of Don and Phil Everly is significant not only for the brothers themselves, but for the music world as a whole. The eternal popularity of the Everlys is one of those musical phenomenons – songs like "Bye, Bye Love" and "Wake Up Little Susie" only seem to grow more poignant and beloved with age. After ten years, the Everlys will be performing those tunes and more as they criss-cross the country on a very special tour.

As Don and Phil roll through their numbers, you're reminded of how many classic songs they wrote and performed, and also of their musical camaraderie with artists such as Bob Dylan and Sam Cooke, whose songs they now render in completely original Everly fashion.

You can tell the boys are glad to be back together. Whether singing exuberantly or looking out over the rehearsal hall, imagining the emotion and excitement that are sure to mark the gigs, the feeling is special. This may be one of the most unforgettable tours ever.

With tender harmonies such as "Bye, Bye Love," "Wake Up Little Susie," and "All I Have to Do Is Dream," the Everly Brothers brought innocence and romance to rock 'n' roll and succeeded as one of the most likable, good-natured and talented singing duos ever to perform before audiences worldwide. Their music was a unique blend of rock 'n' roll, country, rockabilly and bluegrass, an eclectic yet highly accessible sound that appealed to people of all musical tastes. Their contemporaries were seminal rock 'n' rollers like Chuck Berry, Buddy Holly, Elvis Presley and Bill Haley, and their influence has touched artists from The Beatles and Bob Dylan to The Byrds, The Hollies, Crosby, Stills, Nash & Young, Simon & Garfunkel, and more. In fact, one of Paul McCartney's earliest show business endeavors was to team up with his brothers to form an act that featured some of the Everlys' songs. The Everlys have sold more than 20 million singles, 5 million albums, and were the first pop group to be signed to a $1 million recording contract. Without question, the boys from the small town of Brownie, Kentucky have made a monumental mark on the world of popular music.

Don and Phil were born into a musical family. Their father Ike was an influential country guitarist, while Ike's father was a country-style fiddler. With music forever sounding throughout the Everly household, it was not surprising that Don and Phil broke into the entertainment world as mere youngsters, aged 8 and 6, respectively, by appearing frequently on their parents' 1940's radio show. The presence of the musically precocious boys helped *The Everly Family Show* enjoy several successful years, especially on station KMA in Shenandoah, Iowa. But the act was retired in the early 1950's, as the advent of television captured the country's imagination and as Don and Phil grew into skilled and ambitious teenagers who wanted to make music and find fortune on their own.

In 1954, Don and Phil joined thousands of other country-music hopefuls by journeying to Nashville in search of a recording contract. Even though America's country-music boom was in full swing, Don and Phil suffered through two frustrating years. They did record one single for Columbia — "The Sun Keeps Shining" and "Keep A-Lovin' Me" — which was released in 1956, but it did not fare well enough for Columbia to extend the boys' six-month contract. Don and Phil were anything but quitters, though, and they turned to writing songs for other artists, confident that they would soon have another chance in the recording studio. They proved quite talented at this; singer Kitty Wells recorded Don's "Thou Shalt Not Steal," while Phil sold many of his songs to Acuff-Rose, then and now the top music publishing house and management company in Nashville. Still, the boys wanted their own sound, to be their own act.

Wesley Rose arranged for the boys to audition for Archie Bleyer, the one-time musical director of *The Arthur Godfrey Show,* whose recently formed Cadence Records had been successful with pop singer Julius LaRosa and was looking to expand into the country market. Bleyer had seen the Everlys when they first arrived in Nashville, but had felt they did not show enough promise at that juncture to sign them. The second time, however, Bleyer was impressed, and the boys were signed on. Bleyer quickly introduced Don and Phil to the fabled songwriting team of Felice and Boudleaux Bryant, who would in the next few years write many of their best-selling songs. After the phenomenal success of the Everlys' first hit in 1957, "Bye, Bye Love," a song which had been rejected by a multitude of other acts but, when performed by the Everlys, reached Number 2 on the pop charts and Number 1 in the country — Don and Phil were on their way. They experienced a heyday of five frenetic years, from 1957 to 1962, as the reigning kings of popular music, a period in which they produced a hit record every three months and created a repertoire of songs that have been cherished by fans and covered by other artists ever since.

Among the hit singles of their years with Cadence were "Bye, Bye Love," "Wake Up Little Susie," "All I Have to Do Is Dream," "Bird Dog," "Let It Be Me," "'Till I Kissed You," "Take a Message to Mary," and "When Will I Be Loved." Their albums of the time included *Songs Our Daddy Taught Us, Fabulous Style of the Everly Brothers,* and *The Everly Brothers' Best.*

In 1960, the Everlys left Cadence Records and signed with Warner Bros. Records, the new label affording them a wider commercial reach and the opportunity to use more ambitious production techniques. Their first Warner's single, "Cathy's Clown," sold over two million copies and was their all-time best-seller. Other successful songs from their Warner Bros. years included "Lucille," "Temptation," "Walk Right Back," and "Crying in the Rain," plus the albums *A Date with the Everly Brothers, It's Everly Time, Instant Party,* and *Both Sides of an Evening.*

But by 1962, the steady stream of hits had begun to taper off; the single issued that year, "That's Old Fashioned," was their last song to ever reach the Top 10. After a brief stint in the Marines (1961-62), Don and Phil returned to find that the rowdier sounds of the "British Invasion" were all the rage. They continued to make music, and did score some successes—singles like "The Price of Love" and "How Can I Meet Her," and the albums *Rock 'n' Soul, Beat 'n' Soul,* and *Two Yanks in England*—but these were not quite enough to recapture their former glory. It was commonly thought that Sixties audiences were no longer drawn to the type of music the Everlys were best known for. Ironically, many of the successful groups whose renown meant diminishing interest in the Everlys owed much of their very existence to the timeless tunes that Don and Phil had so carefully crafted years before.

Don and Phil were to have another time in the spotlight. Their 1968 album, *Roots,* was an enormous success. In it, the Everlys took a retrospective look at their career, examining where they'd been over the past decade, and even including snippets of music and talk from the old radio show. *Roots* was touching and immensely popular, an achievement that sparked a brief rejuvenation of the Everlys as performers, enough to make the albums that followed—*Stories We Could Tell* and *Pass the Chicken and Listen*—successful as well.

During the next several years, Don and Phil began to go their separate ways; both were experiencing various personal troubles and other pressure stemming mostly from their many years of close proximity and life in the limelight. This unhappy time was punctuated by the brothers' tense appearance at Knotts Berry Farm in July 1973 for what turned out to be their last performance together. Many apocryphal tales have been told of what happened on that day, but what is most clear, amidst the rumors of smashed guitars and broken dreams, was Don's telling the crowd that, "The Everly Brothers died ten years ago." For many, it was the end of an era.

On September 22 and 23, 1983, the Everly Brothers had their long-awaited reunion at London's prestigious Royal Albert Hall. It was a reunion to remember, for fans, for critics and for the Everlys themselves. As music critic Robin Denselow wrote in *The Manchester Guardian:*

"Grand reunions and nostalgia have become a predictable part of the music business in recent years, but last night's stirring, highly emotional event was something truly special. To see a great Sixties band like The Animals together is bizarre, but to see a legend from the Fifties like the Everly Brothers was quite extraordinary, particularly as the years have been kind to their wonderful voices, if not their looks.

"This was their first performance together in ten years, but their greatest period really ended twenty years ago, when Don first retired during a British tour. In the six previous years they'd established themselves as the greatest harmony duo in rock history, and the greatest early exponents of rock's white country roots.

"Last night they came on in dinner jackets as in the early days, with Don, now 46, looking somewhat plump and chubby faced, but with Phil, a year his junior, still as sharp as an old-time country gambler. In the past their off-stage fights were legendary, but now Don claimed "we're friends again" after announcing "with rock 'n' roll you never get old."

"That seems true for their vocals, at least. Backed by their own strummed black acoustic guitars and an excellent five-piece band that included Pete Wingfield on keyboards and the wonderful Albert Lee on guitar, they delivered those clear, whining, chilling harmonies as brilliantly as on their early recordings.

"Staring devotedly at each other, they sounded as happy with the up-tempo rock classics like "Cathy's Clown" and "Wake Up Little Susie" as with the glorious old harmony weepers like "Ebony Eyes" or the country and folk songs they performed with their country musician parents as children. Reunions are rarely this perfect."

The concert was subsequently seen by millions of television viewers throughout the world, including HBO and PBS stations in the United States and the BBC in Britain, and also on home videocassette.

Together again as performers, writers, and brothers, The Everlys toured major American and European cities during the summer of 1984. In addition to re-releases of classic recordings, a new LP, *Everly Brothers '84*, with compositions by such artists as Paul McCartney and Jeff Lynne of ELO fame, was scheduled for release in time for Christmas, 1984.

## test your rock-ability

## WILL THE REAL BALDEMAR HUERTA PLEASE STAND UP?

**Match the performer with his real name:**

A. Ringo Starr
B. Rick James
C. Elvis Costello
D. Freddy Fender
E. Alice Cooper
F. Cat Stevens
G. Elton John
H. Meat Loaf
I. John Denver
J. ? (Question Mark)
K. Muddy Waters
L. Tiny Tim
M. Bob Dylan

1. Declan McManus
2. Vincent Furnier
3. Baldemar Huerta
4. Henry Deutschendorf
5. Marvin Lee Aday
6. McKinley Morganfield
7. Reg Dwight
8. Richard Starkey
9. James Johnson
10. Robert Zimmerman
11. Rudy Martinez
12. Stephen Demetri Georgiou
13. Herbert Buckingham Khaury

# WE GOTTA GET OUT OF THIS PLACE

Match the star with his previous occupation:

A. Elvis Presley
B. Roger Daltrey
C. Jimi Hendrix
D. Ian Dury
E. Chuck Berry
F. Chrissie Hynde
G. Rod Stewart
H. Elvis Costello
I. Deborah Harry
J. Sly Stone
K. Grace Slick
L. Chubby Checker

1. Model
2. Gravedigger
3. Beautician
4. Computer Programmer
5. Paratrooper
6. Truck Driver
7. Chicken Plucker
8. Rock Critic
9. Disc Jockey
10. Sheet Metal Worker
11. Playboy bunny
12. College Professor

Match the star with his or her <u>alma mater</u>:

M. Neil Diamond
N. Mick Jagger
O. Carly Simon
P. Jim Morrison
Q. David Byrne
R. Grace Slick
S. Paul Simon
T. Gram Parsons

13. UCLA
14. Sarah Lawrence College
15. Queens College
16. London School of Economics
17. Finch College
18. New York University
19. Rhode Island School of Design
20. Harvard University

# CELLULOID HEROES

The two medias of rock music and film overlap constantly. Each of these hits made its first appearance in a movie—which movie was it?

**A.** "Nobody Does It Better," Carly Simon
**B.** "Last Dance," Donna Summer
**C.** "Stayin' Alive," The Bee Gees
**D.** "Raindrops Keep Fallin' On My Head," B.J. Thomas
**E.** "Late in the Evening," Paul Simon
**F.** "Eye of the Tiger," Survivor
**G.** "Knockin' On Heaven's Door," Bob Dylan
**H.** "Call Me," Blondie
**I.** "Mrs. Robinson," Simon & Garfunkel
**J.** "Evergreen," Barbra Streisand

On the flip side: Who performed these title songs?

**K.** "Live and Let Die"
**L.** "Endless Love"
**M.** "The Main Event"
**N.** "Grease"
**O.** "Super Fly"
**P.** "9 to 5"
**Q.** "Chariots of Fire"
**R.** "The Goodbye Girl"
**S.** "That's the Way of the World"
**T.** "High School Confidential"

# FREEZE-FRAME

**Which rock group or singer starred in this film?**

1. *Caveman*
2. *Having A Wild Weekend*
3. *Journey Through The Past*
4. *The Song Remains The Same*
5. *200 Motels*
6. *Change of Habit*
7. *The Man Who Fell To Earth*
8. *The Great Rock 'n' Roll Swindle*
9. *Rude Boy*
10. *Renaldo & Clara*
11. *One-Trick Pony*
12. *Union City*
13. *Gimme Shelter*
14. *All You Need Is Cash*
15. *The Harder They Come*
16. *Two-Lane Blacktop*
17. *Rock 'n' Roll High School*
18. *The Fastest Guitar Alive*
19. *The Rose*
20. *Head*

# SELLING OUT

Match the hit with the product it was corrupted to advertise:

1. "California Girls," The Beach Boys
2. "Calendar Girl," Neil Sedaka
3. "Whole Lotta Shakin' Goin On," Jerry Lee Lewis
4. "Light My Fire," The Doors
5. "Anticipation," Carly Simon
6. "Good Vibrations," The Beach Boys
7. "Oh, Pretty Woman," Roy Orbison
8. "The Candy Man," Sammy Davis, Jr.
9. "The Twist," Chubby Checker
10. "Short Shorts," The Royal Teens
11. "Yummy Yummy Yummy," Ohio Express
12. "Up, Up, & Away," The Fifth Dimension
13. "Just One Look," Doris Troy
14. "Still The One," Orleans

A. ABC Television
B. Heinz Ketchup
C. Shakey's Pizza
D. Esskay Meats
E. TWA (Trans World Airlines)
F. Clairol Herbal Essence Shampoo
G. Mazda
H. Sunkist
I. Tone Soap
J. M&Ms
K. Purina Cat Chow
L. Brim Coffee
M. Buick
N. Nair

# BODY LANGUAGE

Drag out your old anatomy textbook and complete these song titles with the appropriate body parts.

1. "Bette Davis _____," Kim Carnes
2. "Our _____ Are Sealed," The Go-Gos
3. "Stop Dragging My _____ Around," Stevie Nicks
4. "Sunshine on My _____," John Denver
5. "_____ —Part 2," Little Stevie Wonder
6. "Hot _____," Rod Stewart
7. "Under My _____," The Rolling Stones
8. "I Want To Hold Your _____," The Beatles
9. "The First Time Ever I Saw Your _____," Roberta Flack
10. "Over My _____," Fleetwood Mac

*The Beatles*

# HELLO, IT'S ME

Identify this artist's first album (U.S. versions only).

1. **Frank Zappa and the Mothers of Invention**
    a. *Freak Out!*
    b. *Absolutely Free*
    c. *The Grand Wazoo*
    d. *Cruising: With Ruben and the Jets*
2. **Billy Joel:**
    a. *Piano Man*
    b. *Streetlife Serenade*
    c. *Cold Spring Harbor*
    d. *Billy Joel*
3. **Elvis Costello:**
    a. *Alison*
    b. *My Aim is True*
    c. *Armed Forces*
    d. *This Year's Model*
4. **Jethro Tull:**
    a. *Stand Up*
    b. *Thick As A Brick*
    c. *This Was*
    d. *Flute of the Room*
5. **Bruce Springsteen:**
    a. *Born to Run*
    b. *Greetings From Asbury Park, N.J.*
    c. *Blinded by the Light*
    d. *The Wild, the Innocent and the E Street Shuffle*

# HELLO, IT'S ME

6. **The Grateful Dead:**
   a. *The Grateful Dead*
   b. *Aoxomoxoa*
   c. *American Beauty*
   d. *Born to Be Dead*

7. **The Police:**
   a. *Regatta de Blanc*
   b. *Zenyatta Mondatta*
   c. *Outlandos D'Amour*
   d. *Magilla Gorilla*

8. **The Beatles:**
   a. *Meet the Beatles!*
   b. *The Beatles*
   c. *The Beatles, England's Newest Hitmakers*
   d. *We're Gonna Change the Face of Pop Music Forever*

9. **Jimi Hendrix:**
   a. *Electric Ladyland*
   b. *Voodoo Chile*
   c. *Cry of Love*
   d. *Are You Experienced?*

10. **Simon and Garfunkel:**
    a. *The Sounds of Silence*
    b. *Parsley, Sage, Rosemary and Thyme*
    c. *Wednesday Morning, 3 A.M.*
    d. *A Poem on the Underground Wall*

# I FOUGHT THE LAW

Each of these performers went to prison, serving sentences that ranged from long to very short. Match the artist with the charge that put him behind bars.

1. Chuck Berry
2. Chuck Berry (second conviction)
3. Arlo Guthrie
4. Chrissie Hynde
5. Paul McCartney
6. Phil Ochs
7. Sid Vicious
8. Mick Jagger and Keith Richards
9. Wendy O. Williams
10. Little Willie John

A. Drunkeness and disorderly conduct
B. Possesssion of drugs
C. Vagrancy
D. Violation of the Mann Act—transporting girls across state lines for immortal porpoises— uh, immoral purposes
E. Murder
F. Onstage obscenity and resisting arrest
G. Possession of marijuana
H. Tax evasion
I. Manslaughter
J. Littering

*Chuck Berry*

# NO BASSIST IN FACT

Here's the bassist—what band does (or did) he play with?

1. John Entwistle
2. Pete Farndon
3. Berry Oakley
4. Tina Weymouth
5. Sid Vicious
6. Roger Waters
7. John Bentley
8. Sting
9. Peter Cetera
10. Chas Chandler

To rephrase things—name the bass player for this band.

11. Led Zeppelin
12. The E Street Band
13. The Clash
14. Creedence Clearwater Revival
15. The Rolling Stones
16. The Go-Gos
17. Fleetwood Mac
18. Yes
19. The Grateful Dead
20. KISS

# answers

## WILL THE REAL BALDEMAR HUERTA PLEASE STAND UP?

**A.** 8
**B.** 9
**C.** 1
**D.** 3 (the <u>real</u> Baldemar Huerta!)
**E.** 2
**F.** 12
**G.** 7
**H.** 5
**I.** 4
**J.** 11
**K.** 6
**L.** 13
**M.** 10

## WE GOTTA GET OUT OF THIS PLACE

**A.** 6
**B.** 10
**C.** 5
**D.** 12 (honestly!)
**E.** 3
**F.** 8
**G.** 2
**H.** 4
**I.** 11
**J.** 9
**K.** 1
**L.** 7
**M.** 18 (on a fencing scholarship)
**N.** 16
**O.** 14 (Sarah Lawrence was also home to Lesley Gore, Linda McCartney, and Yoko Ono)
**P.** 13
**Q.** 19
**R.** 17
**S.** 15
**T.** 20

## CELLULOID HEROES

A. *The Spy Who Loved Me* (the 11th James Bond film)
B. *Thank God It's Friday*
C. *Saturday Night Fever*
D. *Butch Cassidy and the Sundance Kid*
E. *One-Trick Pony,* written and starred in by Simon
F. *Rocky III*
G. *Pat Garrett and Billy the Kid* (in which Dylan plays "Alias")
H. *American Gigolo*
I. *The Graduate*
J. *A Star is Born* (Streisand also wrote the music)
K. Paul McCartney and Wings
L. Diana Ross and Lionel Richie
M. Barbra Streisand
N. Frankie Valli (minus the 4 Seasons: song written by Barry Gibb)
O. Curtis Mayfield
P. Dolly Parton
Q. Vangelis
R. David Gates (without Bread)
S. Earth, Wind, & Fire
T. Jerry Lee Lewis (his last hit before being blacklisted for marrying his 13-year-old cousin Myra Gale)

# FREEZE-FRAME

1. Ringo Starr
2. The Dave Clark Five—who, strangely, do not sing or play on camera in this film by John Boorman (he went on to do *Deliverance* and *Excalibur*, to name two)
3. Neil Young
4. Led Zeppelin
5. Frank Zappa (also features Ringo Starr and Flo & Eddie)
6. Elvis Presley, as a doctor who tempts nun Mary Tyler Moore to cast off her whimple
7. David Bowie, who astonished critics and fans with his fine performance
8. The Sex Pistols and their manager, the outrageous Malcolm McLaren
9. The Clash
10. Bob Dylan—his excruciating home movies of the 1976 Rolling Thunder Revue
11. Paul Simon, who also wrote the screenplay
12. Deborah Harry of Blondie, with brown hair
13. The Rolling Stones, with particular emphasis on Mick
14. The Rutles—a loving Beatles parody with an appearance by George
15. Reggae sensation Jimmy Cliff
16. James Taylor (Dennis Wilson also attempts to act here)
17. The Ramones
18. Roy Orbison
19. Bette Midler, doing a thinly disguised Janis Joplin
20. The Monkees, with a cameo appearance by Frank Zappa. The stars appear in one sequence as dandruff in the hair of Victor Mature.

# SELLING OUT

1. *F* ("Wish they all could be Herbal Essence girls...")
2. *K* ("I love I love I love my calendar cat...")
3. *C* ("Whole lotta Shakey's goin' on...")
4. *M* ("Come on, Buick, light my fire...")
5. *B* (They didn't have to change anything)
6. *H* ("I'm soaking up good vibrations, Sunkist is a taste sensation...")
7. *I*
8. *J* ("The M&Ms man...")
9. *L* ("Let's do the Brim twist...")
10. *N* ("If you dare wear shorts shorts, Nair for short shorts...")
11. *D* ("Yummy yummy yummy, got Esskay in my tummy...")
12. *E* ("Up, up, and away, TWA...")
13. G
14. *A* ("You're still having fun, and we're still the one")

**EXTRA CREDIT:** *"I'd Like to Teach the World to Sing,"* which started life as *"I'd Like to Buy the World a Coke."*

# BODY LANGUAGE

1. Eyes
2. Lips
3. Heart
4. Shoulder
5. Fingertips
6. Legs
7. Thumb
8. Hand
9. Face
10. Head

# HELLO, IT'S ME

1. *Freak Out!*
2. *Cold Spring Harbor.* Joel's first album was mastered at the wrong speed, leading some to speculate that Alvin of the Chipmunks had finally released a solo album.
3. *My Aim Is True*
4. *This Was*
5. *Greetings From Asbury Park, N.J.*, which failed commercially after an attempt to promote Springsteen as "the new Bob Dylan" backfired.
6. *The Grateful Dead*
7. *Outlandos D'Amour.* They didn't *really* make an album called *Magilla Gorilla.*
8. *Meet the Beatles!* was their first American release; *The Beatles* is the official name of the record universally called "The White Album"; it was actually the Rolling Stones' first album that was credited to "England's Newest Hitmakers"; and *We're Gonna Change the Face of Pop Music Forever* is the name of the Beatles' first album in Mark Shipper's satirical Beatle fantasy, *Paperback Writer.*
9. *Are You Experienced?*
10. *Wednesday Morning, 3 A.M.*, featuring the original acoustic version of "The Sounds of Silence."

# I FOUGHT THE LAW

1. *D* (Berry's first tragic conviction was little more than a frame-up)
2. *H* (Berry's second tragic conviction, unfortunately, was not)
3. *J*
4. *A*

5. *G* (Japanese customs authorities arrested Paul at the airport, leading to the cancellation of his Japanese tour)
6. *C*
7. *E* (Vicious died of a heroin OD while awaiting trial for the murder of girlfriend Nancy Spungen)
8. *B* (The Glimmer Twins released their sardonic "We Love You" upon their release)
9. *F*
10. *I* (John, who had the original hit with "Fever" when Peggy Lee was still in bobby sox, died of pneumonia in prison)

# NO BASSIST IN FACT

1. The Who
2. The Pretenders
3. The Allman Brothers Band
4. The Talking Heads (extra credit for her solo project, the Tom Tom Club)
5. The Sex Pistols
6. Pink Floyd
7. Squeeze
8. The Police
9. Chicago
10. The Animals. Chandler later managed Jimi Hendrix.
11. John Paul Jones, who also played keyboards
12. Garry Tallent
13. Paul Simonon
14. Stu Cook
15. The stalwart Bill Wyman
16. Kathy Valentine
17. John McVie, whose name provides the group Fleetwood with their Mac
18. Chris Squire
19. Phil Lesh
20. Gene Simmons, the guy who spits blood and stuff like that

# SPECIAL BONUS FEATURE:

## solo career

The very first reviews of the Jackson Five speculated dubiously about what the future might hold for a group of cute black kids whose music appealed primarily to the bubblegum set. Most of the predictions were gloomy, but there was one exception: It was generally agreed that whatever happened to the Jacksons as a group, Michael was a good bet for a long career as a solo artist.

Well, they were wrong about the fate of the Jackson Five, but they were certainly right about Michael. Today his solo career is the most successful in the world.

Michael's first solo effort was an album he made back in 1972, called *Got To Be There*. The idea of a solo album for Michael came primarily from Motown. They wanted to capitalize on his popularity as the lead singer of the Jackson Five, and they may also have intended a hedge for the future, in case it turned out to be true that the Jackson Five would lose their audience once they all grew up.

They turned Michael over to veteran Motown producer Hal Davis, and the ubiquitous "Corporation," and waited to see what would happen. What did was a hit single, a successful album, and an award for Male Vocalist of the Year. Quite a feat for a thirteen-year-old boy's debut album.

The single was "Got To Be There," a bouncy love song. *Rolling Stone*'s Vince Aletti commented, "On 'Got To Be There,' Michael's voice echoes and swirls, whispers and cries out with this unbelievable purity: 'Ooh, what a feeling there'll be/the moment she says she loves me.' It's a weird combination of innocence and utter professionalism, real feeling and careful calculation, that's fascinating and finally irresistible." The single made it all the way to the Number 1 spot on the charts, as hordes of teenyboppers fueled their daydreams of a romance with Michael Jackson.

Another single from this album also did well, and has since become a Jackson standard at concerts, and that was "Rockin' Robin." Later, one more cut from the album got airplay as a single, "I Wanna Be Where You Are." Aletti characterized it as a "supreme production, with shouting from

Michael that equals his early work and a finish that always has me screaming loud enough to alarm the neighbors." The critic concluded, "Even the inconsequential songs on Michael's album have their appeal." All in all, it was an impressive first solo performance. His peers in the music business agreed, a fact which they demonstrated by voting him the Best Male Vocalist of the Year on the strength of his performance on "Got To Be There."

Motown was never a company to refrain from striking while the iron was hot. Not only did they set in motion another album, but they arranged for Michael to sing the theme song for a movie that was expected to appeal to the same young people who bought his records. The movie was *Ben*, a low-budget horror flick that was well calculated to appeal to the fantasies of pre-pubescents. The hero is a boy who is spurned by his classmates. His scheme for revenge on the whole heartless world involves breeding ferocious rats who are going to do his bidding. The leader is a large rat named Ben, who becomes the boy's best friend.

As you can tell from this brief plot summary, the title song, "Ben," an ode to the boy's rat friend, could easily turn into terrible bathos or a bad joke. But Michael Jackson brought to this little ballad his own special quality of innocence and belief, and he made it a touching experience. Critic Vince Aletti admitted that Michael's delivery of the lines "They don't see you as I do / I wish they would try to" tore him up every time he heard it. Michael's rendition of this title song became a hit single; he was asked to sing it at the Academy Awards presentation, and Motown also made it the title song of his next album, which features a picture of Michael and a rat on the cover. The title song more or less carried the album, which had no other hit single and no particularly memorable songs in the Michael Jackson canon.

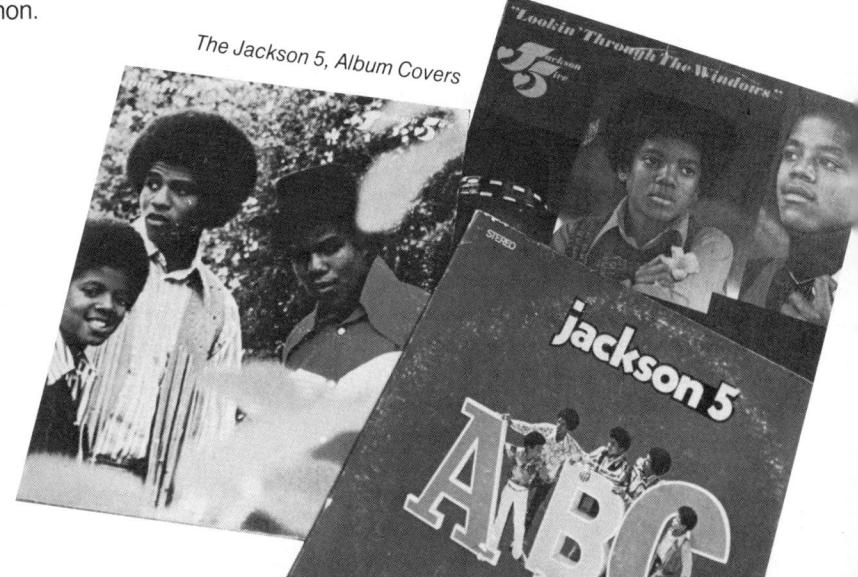

*The Jackson 5, Album Covers*

Michael didn't make another solo album until early in 1975. Motown decided to turn their young star over to one of their most successful producers, Brian Holland. He had worked for Motown in the early years, and was largely responsible for the sound of the Supremes; then he left to form his own production company, Holland-Dozier-Holland Production, Inc. Now he had signed a contract with Motown for a return engagement, to produce a new album for the Supremes, one for the Jackson Five (Moving Violation) and a solo album for Michael.

The album was called *Forever, Michael*. It tried to build on Michael's more mature voice and his more mainstream style (this was about the time that the Jacksons were appearing in Vegas and at Radio City Music Hall). There is some difference of opinion about the result.

Some people felt that the album was artistically successful, even though neither of its two singles had the sales one might expect for a star of Michael's magnitude. This school of thought blames the album's commercial insignificance on the fact that it was released after the Jacksons had announced the move to Epic. They point out that Motown had neither the motive nor the inclination to promote the album the way they had his past production. Vince Aletti described "Just a Little Bit of You," one of the singles released, as "a wonderfully bouncy, romantic prescription with a driving intro and cascades of violins that put Barry White and MFSB to shame." The other single was "Dear Michael," a saccharine little ballad based on an imaginary letter from a fan who closed by predicting sadly that he'll never, ever see her letter; Michael responds by saying he is dreaming of meeting her and signs himself, "Forever, Michael." It *is* all a bit too cute, although as usual Michael manages to put the lyrics over with convincing sincerity.

The other school of thought denounced *Forever, Michael* as a flop because it was too slick, too pop, too far away from Michael's roots. The reviewer for *High Fidelity* complained that the album had gone too far into the middle-of-the-road. "Yes, Jackson is an expert ballad singer; yes, this disc with its many famous producers is slicker than slick; yes, it is attractive and entertaining. Nevertheless, I object to this conventional treatment of an unconventional talent. The de-souling of Michael Jackson may be one way to lengthen his career. But it's a sad route to take."

Now that we can view *Forever, Michael* within the context of Michael Jackson's career to date, it seems a natural step in his evolution into the mainstream of popular music. His first two albums drew heavily on the rhythm-and-blues background that had been the foundation of the Jackson Five's musical experience; Motown contributed an element of slickly packaged soul. But if Michael Jackson had simply continued to record in that mold, he would have appealed to a limited audience—mostly blacks—

and he would have failed to grow artistically. Already, in his earlier songs such as "Ben," "Got To Be There," and "We've Got a Good Thing Going," Michael had proved conclusively that he was capable of putting across a ballad, handling material that touched the audience emotionally—often at the very same moment that it made them want to dance. On *Forever, Michael*, he simply extended this range with cuts like the title song, "Take Me Back" and "One Day in Your Life." As a whole, the album is perhaps a bit too slick, a bit too glitzy. But it was a necessary step along the way to the pop sound eventually perfected by Michael Jackson that is a fusion of pop romanticism with the driving beat of dance music.

Right after Michael left Motown, that record label brought out its last Michael Jackson album, *The Best of Michael Jackson*. It went back into the Jackson catalog to pull out some of Michael's hottest songs, both with and without the Jackson Five. Considering the small amount of promotion it received, it sold reasonably well, but basically the album was created without the involvement of Michael.

The next step for Michael's growth as a recording artist came when the Jacksons were finally able to write and produce their own music, in the creation of the *Destiny* album. Michael had been writing songs steadily for several years, but this was his first chance to work them out in the recording studio, to try to advance them from the sound in his head to the same sound on the master tape. He co-wrote, with brother Randy, the hit song "Shake Your Body (Down to the Ground)" and he also was responsible for its unusual sound. Arranger and keyboard player Greg Phillinganes remembers being impressed by the originality of the effects Michael finally produced, especially toward the end of the song, when vocals and most instruments fade out, to leave only the insistent rhythm of the synthesizer bass and drums to carry the dancers through to the end of the record. He told a reporter, "The long instrumental tag on 'Shake' was totally their idea. I played on the record, but hadn't heard the final version. Michael handed me a copy of the test pressing and with his big smile said, 'Listen to this.' Well, it was hot!"

Another song on *Destiny* that is significant in Michael's career development is the tune called "Bless His Soul," written by Michael and (he now confirms) written *about* him as well. Here we begin for the first time to penetrate into the inner world of Michael Jackson, where innocence and the desire to love are threatened by the acts of a hostile world—or the fear of that hostility. One verse, for example, goes, "Sometimes I cry cause I'm confused/Is this a fact of being used?/There is no life for me at all/'Cause I give myself at beck and call." Subsequently in his solo albums (and especially in *Thriller*), Michael would continue to explore this inner territory, exposing some basic uneasiness about the intentions of the world in which he must live—a feeling that obviously strikes a chord in many of his listeners.

*Destiny* gave Michael a chance to hone his skills in songwriting and record producing, but he was still looking for more creative freedom. Recording with a group, even when they're all your brothers and have worked with you for more than a decade, is always slightly confining, because things must be agreed upon jointly, worked out ahead of time, altered to allow for the strengths and weaknesses of the group members. Michael felt it was time for another solo album.

And when he met Quincy Jones while acting in *The Wiz*, he knew he had found the right producer to work with. The two of them had hit it off from the very start. Quincy told a reporter, "Michael's a truth machine. He's got a balance between the wisdom of a 60-year-old and the enthusiasm of a child." And Michael in his turn respected Quincy's professional accomplishments. Quincy was a trumpet player who had once played with the great Ray Charles band. In the 1960's, he began to produce some successful pop singles (one of the best known is "It's My Party" by Leslie Gore). A multi-talented man, he also put together his own jazz band, and did successful live performances and recordings. In the 1970's, he began to get involved in music for films and TV, and was the musical director for *Roots*—and, of course, *The Wiz*.

Quincy Jones had the reputation of a producer who knew how to get what he wanted in the studio. He was identified with a classy, smooth sound; it's the kind of music that sounds simple and relaxed when you first hear it but that later reveals itself to be full of complexity and sophistication. When the executives at Epic heard that Michael wanted "Q" to produce his next album, they all became a bit nervous. How would Michael's raw energy and rhythm-and-blues-based music mesh with Quincy's jazz sounds and smooth veneer?

The answer turned out to be, very well. The album that they created together, called *Off the Wall*, was an unprecedented hit. It sold over seven million copies worldwide (*Destiny*, which Epic certainly regarded as a success, in comparison sold a mere one million copies). Two singles from the album made it to the Number 1 spot — "Don't Stop 'Til You Get Enough," and "Rock with You." This total of four hit singles from one album was a record for a solo album (it had been equalled just once before by a group, Fleetwood Mac, with their monster album *Rumours*). Just for good measure, Michael threw in a fifth song that became a top-selling single in the UK, although never in the US: "Girlfriend." Michael also won a Grammy for Best Male Rhythm-and-Blues performer for his vocal on "Don't Stop 'Til You Get Enough."

*Off the Wall* was released at a time that the record business seemed to be going into a slump, and it was one of the few bright spots on the financial horizon for many record store owners during 1979 and 1980. In fact, it continued to sell throughout 1981, and was voted most popular soul album for that year by readers of *Cash Box*, a music-business trade paper. But its success was not limited to its commercial aspect alone. Most critics agreed that it was an artistic triumph — for Michael Jackson as well as all the other musicians who worked with him.

Once again Michael Jackson demonstrated his talent as a songwriter. He wrote the hit "Don't Stop 'Til You Get Enough," which is one of the best pieces of dance music ever created. An interesting sidelight on Michael's method of writing this type of song, in which the rhythm is such an integral part of the effect, is that he says he writes on piano and drum — an unusual approach, but perhaps it helps to explain his ultimate success. For many songwriters, the beat is something that is added later, often at the behest of an arranger or producer who is trying to flesh out the melody and chord structure that the writer has come up with. In Michael's case, through his use of the drum, that all-important element of the beat is already there, worked in and around the words and the music. It assures that the lyrics "speak" the right way, that the phrases of the melody start and end in the right places, that the entire composition is propelled by the beat rather than merely adorned by it.

Michael wrote another cut on the album as well, "Working Day and Night." Gerri Hirshey, writing about Michael in *Rolling Stone*, commented aptly that this song could only have been written by a dancer. Its sense of pace is truly incredible, and it's true that it does seem to have built into it those places for just the right spin, or twist, or funky little rhythm step, that give a dance its punctuation.

Other writers helped with *Off the Wall* too. Both the title cut and the other big hit, "Rock with You," were written by Rod Temperton (formerly a member of Heat Wave and also the writer of George Benson's big hit, "Give Me the Night"). Temperton also contributed "Burn This Disco Out," a good piece of dance music. Paul McCartney was another contributor, penning the song "Girlfriend" which was such a success in the UK.

Of course, the song itself is only the beginning. The real challenge is putting it over — singing it in a way that makes the listener *hear* the lyrics and feel the melody and beat. And no one in the world is better than Michael Jackson at either of these tasks. Part of his effectiveness comes from the fact that it is obvious that he is himself strongly affected by the song. He told one reporter that when he sang "Don't Stop 'Til You Get Enough" he felt touched by a force within. "The thing that touches me is very special. It's a message I have to tell. I start crying and the pain is wonderful. It's amazing. It's like God."

And Quincy Jones remembers the struggle he had because of Michael's involvement with the music on one particular cut, the beautiful and sad ballad, "She's Out of My Life." He said, "I had a song I'd been saving for Michael called 'She's Out of My Life' [written by Tom Bahler]. Michael heard it, and it clicked. But when he sang it, he would cry. Every time we did it, I'd look up at the end and Michael would be crying. I said, 'We'll come back in two weeks and do it again, and maybe it won't tear you up so much.' Came back and he started to get teary. So we left it in." Clearly, when the singer feels the mood of the song so strongly, the listener is going to be drawn into that emotion. And Michael, because he seems to be such a believer himself, so totally devoid of cynicism, can virtually make an audience share his tears.

*Off the Wall* also marked another step in Michael's development as a producer, since he continued on this album to be involved in the process that turns a song into a finished recording. Quincy Jones praised his willingness to work and learn: "He does his homework and rehearses and works hard at home. Most singers want to do everything in the studio. They're lazy.... When he commits to an idea, he goes all the way with it.... It's a long way from idea to execution. Everybody wants to go to heaven and nobody wants to die." Michael was an exception – and an exception especially rare among singers.

The way modern studio recordings are made tends to encourage a singer to remain uninvolved with the rest of the music. Commonly, the producer and/or arranger begins the process with a group of studio musicians. They start by having a piano player beat out the rhythm and the melody and anybody who feels like it singing the vocal part; this is captured on one track of the tape and later erased. Then, as the musicians listen to this skeleton tape, they begin to lay down tracks on top of it. Usually the drums and bass go first, then the keyboards, then lead instrumentals, such as the guitar breaks, or the wailing saxophone, or the synthesizer tricks. Each of these instruments will probably be recorded on a separate track, which makes it easy to replace or rework any of them (and is quite feasible in the modern recording studio with its 32- or even 48-track capacity).

Once the entire instrumental part of the recording is more or less complete, the star vocalist comes into the studio – often without a single live musician in there with him. He puts on the earphones and listens to the music that has already been created. Then he simply sings along with it, and his work is done. He goes home to count his future royalties and autograph his glossies.

Meanwhile, back in the studio, the producer and the engineer mix the master tape making critical decisions about how loud each instrumental track should be, how much treble or bass on each single instrument, how far above the instrumental the vocal should be pitched. They may decide to make some changes, by re-recording an instrumental part, overdubbing another instrument, hiring some back-up singers to thicken the vocal texture, inserting an echo here, a fadeout there. In short, using the raw material of the taped tracks, they create the album. Then they send a test pressing to the star, who listens to it a few times to find out what's on it and then runs out to tell everyone about "my" new record.

But with Michael Jackson, things are very different. To begin with, he has written some of the songs. In the second place, he has jammed with the musicians who are going to play on the record to get some musical ideas stirred up, and then he has rehearsed with them to work those ideas out. He is likely to be in the studio while they record their tracks—and if he isn't, he is going to have those tracks messengered right over to his house, where he will listen to them in his own recording studio to decide what works and what doesn't. By the time he actually begins to record himself, he is thoroughly in command of the musical creation. And then he will sit in the studio for hours listening to the mixing process, helping to decide what the final sound should be. Once there is a final master tape, Michael will also be involved in checking the test pressing for quality and fidelity, approving the album cover and sleeve, reading over the promotional material and the planned advertising for the album. In fact, he will continue to monitor all the activities involved in marketing and selling the album, right up until the day when he checks over the accountants' audit of Epic's records of number of copies of the album sold and royalties due.

Anyone who has worked with him has come to recognize that, professionally, Michael Jackson is in full control. Steven Spielberg elucidated, "Sometimes he appears to other people to be sort of wavering on the fringes of twilight, but there is great conscious forethought behind everything he does. He's very smart about his career and the choices he makes." And Greg Phillinganes, who once again worked with Michael as keyboardist on *Off the Wall*, spoke more specifically about the way Michael collaborated in the studio with producer Quincy Jones. "Their ideas just blend into each other. You see, Michael is not like a lot of other singers who came around just to add a vocal. Michael is involved in the whole album. 'Q' is basically an overseer who runs the show without really running the show."

*Off the Wall* was a major triumph for Michael Jackson. The album stayed on the Top 10 for nearly eight months, and altogether made the charts for 84 weeks. It went Platinum in the US, UK, Australia and Canada; in Holland it merely went Gold. And it spawned five hit singles worldwide. For some artists, such an album would be the highlight of a lifetime. But for Michael, it was just a warm-up for bigger things to come.

For the next two years, Michael put most of his working time into The Jacksons, making the album *Triumph* and going out on tour with a show that was largely his own creation. But by 1982, he was ready to work on his own again.

He began the year by writing a song for his friend Diana Ross. Titled "Muscles," it was downright steamy in its sexuality, a woman's plea for a great male body to hold on to. (Amusingly, the title is also the name of Michael's pet boa constrictor, a great body that wants to hold onto *you*.) When he brought the song to Diana, she loved its theatricality, but told Michael she would record it on one condition only: that he act as producer of the song. He suggested that they should co-produce it, but she stood firm in demanding that he should take full responsibility in the studio. He agreed, they made the record, it was released as a single. It was a shot in the arm for Diana's recording career, and became a hit on both the pop and the rhythm-and-blues charts.

Before he turned to work on his own new solo album, Michael took the time to record another collaboration, this time with Paul McCartney. He sang a duet with Paul on a tune called "Say, Say, Say" and another one, "The Man." Both were contained on Paul's new album, and "Say, Say, Say" was released as a single (in 1983) that made the charts in both the US and the UK. While he and Paul were working together, they went on to cut a track for Michael's new album as well. The song was called "The Girl Is Mine" and it's an argument between Paul and Michael over the affections of a young lady.

With the work with Paul behind him, it was time for Michael to settle down and do the hard work to create his next solo album, to be called *Thriller*. Once again, he chose to have Quincy Jones produce the album—why quarrel with success?—and Quincy also contributed one song that he co-wrote, "PYT (Pretty Young Thing)"; it was recorded with Michael's sisters LaToya and Janet singing back-up. Rod Temperton was back too, writing the title song as well as two other tracks on the album, "The Lady in My Life" and "Baby Be Mine." But in addition to going back to the people who helped make *Off the Wall* such a success, Michael also brought in some new musical talent. The rock group Toto plays back-up on several cuts, and one of their members, Steve Porcaro, co-wrote the strong song "Human Nature." Drummer Ndugu Chanceler came in to lay down a drum track on "Billie Jean," and heavy-metal guitarist Eddie Van Halen agreed to contribute a long solo on "Beat It." The master of horror, Vincent Price, dropped by to tape a silly horror rap for the conclusion of *Thriller*. This willingness to collaborate with other well-known artists, to ask them to contribute the things they do best, is the mark of a mature artist.

Michael himself wrote three of the songs on *Thriller*, and they too are a sign of his continuing development as an artist. What's interesting about all three of them is the way they combine a bouncy upbeat rhythm with lyrics that are darkly brooding, even paranoid, in their feeling. "Beat It" is a song about gang warfare, and it seems to explore man's potential for violence. The singer keeps advocating peace — "don't wanna see no blood" — but it is obvious that others are thrusting violence upon him. In "Billie Jean," he talks about a paternity suit of which the singer is the victim; again, it seems that other people are creating situations that the singer finds intolerable. "Wanna Be Startin' Somethin'" is perhaps the most explicit of the three songs, with its denunciation of gossiping tongues and its acknowledgment of their power to hurt the singer. The singer calls himself a "buffet," a "vegetable" — in other words, something to be devoured by others, all of whom have hostile motives. Lyrics like these suggest that being Michael Jackson is not, despite the money and the success, all fun and games. But the artistry lies not in the complaint, but in Michael's ability to fuse the complaint with the music and to create something that simultaneously makes you dance and makes you think.

When it came to recording the three songs he wrote himself, Michael shared production chores with Quincy Jones. For the rest of the cuts, he was, as usual, deeply involved with the creation of the record, but Quincy was once again the person with ultimate control. There is no question but that *Thriller* is a heavily produced album — the creation of countless hours spent manipulating tracks in the studio rather than the spontaneous effort of a group of musicians getting together to play something. But the net effect is still one of simplicity. The complexity and sophistication are there, but they are not intrusive. A perfect example can be seen in the drum sound in "Billie Jean." According to drummer Chanceler, "Michael always knew how he wanted it to sound. There was originally just a drum machine track on it. I came in and cut a live drum track over the overdub, so that at times during the record there is just me and then the two together." To the casual listener, all that is apparent is the steady rhythmic shuffle. But the variety of that sound appeals to more sophisticated listeners and — just as important — it makes the song hold up under frequent playing, whereas a simple drum machine alone might get monotonous after you'd heard it a few times.

This ability to stand up under repeated listening is no doubt one of the strengths of *Thriller* and one of the reasons that it has been so phenomenally successful. The numbers tell the story. *Thriller* was the best-selling album of 1983, selling (to date) nearly 35 million copies worldwide — and still, as of this writing, in the Number 1 spot. Perhaps even more amazing is the fact that six — yes, six — of the songs on the album have become best-selling singles. This record is unprecedented; and when you consider that the album has only nine songs on it to begin with, you realize that two-thirds of the songs are singles hits!

*Thriller* has been a truly international success. The album went Platinum in the US, Canada, UK, Holland, Australia, New Zealand, Japan, Germany, France, Sweden, Belgium, Switzerland, Spain, Greece and South Africa; it went Gold in Denmark, Italy, Israel and Norway.

And its success is not just financial, but artistic as well. John Rockwell characterized *Thriller* as a "wonderful pop record" and "another signpost on the road to Michael Jackson's own artistic fulfillment." Vince Aletti, who has been covering Michael Jackson from the very beginning of his career, said, "Here, Quincy gracefully opens the door and the real Michael Jackson steps through: Mr. Entertainment. Obviously, Michael's been honing his art along with his ambition and the result is remarkably sharp, intensely focused...." It was widely agreed that Michael's achievement on the album put him in the category of major pop artists.

And *Thriller*'s success also had a major impact on the record industry. Some people go so far as to claim that Michael has rejuvenated the music business. The enormous profitability of *Thriller* has made the record companies bullish again, willing to risk money discovering new artists and developing old ones, in the hope of finding another *Thriller*. Moreover, retailers believe that the sales of *Thriller* created additional sales as well; people who came into the record stores to buy the Michael Jackson album frequently picked up something else while they were there.

But it's not just in record sales alone that Michael Jackson has pointed the way to the future. It is also in synthesizing a new appeal to a wider music audience. For black artists, the success of both of Michael's albums is encouraging, because it proves that black performers can sell records in large quantities — a question that many people in the record business used to debate. And it means that music with its roots in the black community can appeal to everyone. Back in the heyday of Motown, and in the early days of rock, black music was recognized to have a wide appeal. But somehow things changed again in the 1970's, and black performers began to fade away as their sounds were taken over by white players (especially English groups) and the origins of the sounds were forgotten. Although Michael Jackson's stage persona is not stereotypically black, his music remains firmly within the black tradition that was his own starting point. A professor of political science who was interviewed in *The New York Times*, Marshall Berman, called Michael the "Al Jolson of the Eighties.... Like Al Jolson, he's bringing black music to a white audience. And like Jolson, he shows that you can come out of the ghetto and if you have the energy, you can do anything. It's the American dream."

Michael's mastery of the American dream has had its good effect on other black musicians. Such performers as Prince and Eddie Grant find that it's much easier to get airplay than it used to be, that there's more interest in an indigenous black sound outside what used to be a limited black audience.

Another aspect of Michael's synthesis of several different styles of music is that the singles hits from *Thriller* have been played on a lot of different kinds of radio stations. Of course they were big hits on the dance-oriented stations, found in the large cities and having as their primary market urban, black young people. But they've also been played on AOR (Album Oriented Rock) stations that have traditionally limited themselves to heavy rock performers and ignored pop and disco releases. An exec of Epic Records confirmed that *Thriller* got a lot of airplay on AOR stations and that it was the first time any Michael Jackson music had made it on those stations. With today's new "narrowcasting" approach to radio, station profits have gone up but performers' opportunities have declined. Many stations are locked into rigid formulas that make it impossible for any artist to move outside his or her "assigned" category. With *Thriller*, Michael Jackson reminded station programming directors that their categories are to a great extent artificial, and that good music can appeal to everyone. A lot of other artists stand to benefit from this reminder.

Can Michael Jackson top *Thriller*? On the face of it, it would seem virtually impossible. But a new album is already in the planning stages. Nothing is yet definite, but Michael has been talking about some new collaborations that will take him even farther into new territory. He wants to record a duet with Freddie Mercury, the lead singer of Queen; he wants to work with Barbra Streisand and with Johnny Mathis; he'll probably work again with Paul McCartney and with Toto.

And he's still writing songs... and moving deeper and deeper inside himself to do it. In fact, he says that many of his songs come to him in dreams, springing up from the deep well of the unconscious. "I wake up from dreams and go 'Wow, put *this* down on paper.' The whole thing is strange. You hear the words, everything is right there in front of your face. And you say to yourself, 'I'm sorry, I just didn't write this. It's there already.' That's why I hate to take credit for the songs I've written. I feel that somewhere, someplace, it's been done and I'm just a courier bringing it into the world."

Well, wherever he gets his inspirations, they're still coming. And the chances are that by the time they reach the audience in the form of an album, Michael's talent and hard work will have turned it into another hit-studded production. You can count on it, Michael won't stop 'til he gets enough.